P9-DDW-219

# Research in Pastoral Care and Counseling
## *Quantitative and Qualitative Approaches*

by
Larry VandeCreek
Hilary E. Bender
Merle R. Jordan

With a Foreword by
Margot Hover

Journal of Pastoral Care Publications, Inc.
©1994

# RESEARCH IN PASTORAL CARE AND COUNSELING: QUANTITATIVE AND QUALITATIVE APPROACHES

©1994
Journal of Pastoral Care Publications, Inc.

ISBN 0-929670-10-8

# Contents

89590

# Acknowledgments

The authors would like to thank *Scientific American* for permission to reprint Figure C on page 80, which appeared in the article, "Subjective Contours," by Gaetano Kanisza. The implied triangle was contributed by Illel Arbel. Figures A, B, and C, appearing on pages 79-80, are reproduced with the permission of Gardner Press, publishers of *Can You Believe Your Eyes?* by J. R. Block and H. E. Yuker.

We especially would like to acknowledge the major contribution to Part Two made by James Barbaria, Ph.D. He met regularly with the authors of that section and provided considerable guidance in helping them to understand the historical and philosophical foundations of qualitative research.

# Foreword

I t's amazing how timely this book is. I suspect that I am fairly typical of
chaplains. When my career began, many departments had established priori-
ties. In some hospitals, chaplains attended all deaths. At others, they visited all
newly admitted patients or all pre-surgery patients or all those of particular
religious denominations. Beyond that, we operated largely on intuition, visiting
patients we felt "called to," or who "looked" as though they could use a visit.

But by the late 1970s, numbers began to be important. Health care facilities were forced to look at efficiency and cost effectiveness. Administrators
competed for Certificates of Need for new facilities and equipment. Positions
and departments were created to monitor quality assurance. Pastoral Care
departments were generally exempt from QA activities, perhaps under the
assumption that requiring accountability would be slightly sacrilegious, or that
God's grace could not be reduced to numbers. Before long, however, health
care facilities of all kinds were being restructured, with priority given to
marketable and reimbursable services. "God's grace" did not rank high on many
lists. And so departments in some institutions were summarily closed, while
others were cut back drastically, leaving us out in the cold with our dedication
and our intuition.

At the same time, however, there were some curious souls who pursued
their curiosity and intuition even onto sacred ground. Some were nudged by
administrators who wanted to keep pastoral services but needed numbers to
justify the cost. Others were convinced that some truths can be known only or
best by systematic research. Some Clinical Pastoral Education programs structured residents' advanced specialty around required research projects.
Meanwhile, some pastoral clinicians and educators explored their own research
interests. For instance, exactly what did our students learn in the course of a

unit of CPE? Was there a correlation between denomination and parishioners' expectations of their pastors? Or between physicians' medical specialties and their expectations and apprehensions of the chaplain's role?

At the risk of over generalizing, before the mid-1980s, writers in pastoral education, care, and counseling tended to rely heavily on anecdotal data to prove their points. In comparison with other behavioral sciences, they were less likely to organize their findings and reflections along the lines of traditional quantitative research—e.g., stating hypothesis, using sampling methods, controls, and statistical tests. This was reassuring to those who were afraid of numbers or felt they lacked the time to collect and organize other kinds of data. Narratives have a different flavor to them than questionnaire responses of yes/no and always/never, and thus were probably more palatable. In the past few years, however, chaplains and pastoral counselors have been challenged by researchers in other disciplines to look seriously at quantitative research methods and their usefulness for their fields. We've found that it is possible to pinpoint the correlation between pastoral visits and length of hospital stay or use of pain medication, for example. We have also been challenged to look again at qualitative research and its applicability to the questions about which we are curious. Are there issues that can be explored best by a combination of both approaches in dialogue with each other? Or is there yet another approach that belongs uniquely to research in pastoral arts and sciences?

Finally, I see two continuing trends involving pastoral research. Four years ago, I submitted my first protocol to our center's Institutional Review Board. It was given an expedited review by the chair. In my anxiety about the whole process, I was grateful not to have to face the entire committee. But I also recognized the possibility that chaplains were viewed as innocuous friendly visitors who could do no harm with a little questionnaire here and there. The next year, we began requiring our residents to do research projects, and the IRB decided to give them all a full review. Despite the pressure of the closer scrutiny, I felt this indicated that our research was being taken as seriously as a drug study or an experimental procedure trial. But it also precipitated a heated discussion by the whole committee on the validity of qualitative research. The learning went both ways; we were challenged to tighten our research designs, and the committee expanded its acceptance both of qualitative methods and of pastoral research itself.

That leads to the second trend I see. Researchers in a whole variety of fields are looking at factors that traditionally have been defined as our realm. Psychologists are looking at religiosity as it affects death anxiety, for instance. Several years ago, a cardiologist told me he was fairly certain that undertaking serious research on the place of spirituality in cardiac rehabilitation would jeopardize his academic career. Within this brief period, he already feels that the climate for his work has grown more favorable. Last week, I spent an afternoon with a business school faculty member who is interested in researching some facet of the impact of spirituality on bedside health care. I recently came upon a list of six or eight researchers in my institution who met over their common interest in quality of life studies a number of years ago. In attempting to resurrect that group, I discovered that its current size would be unwieldy; *everyone* is interested in quality of life research these days! Another example: one hospital is sponsoring a regional institute on research for nurses, physicians, chaplains, social workers, and other health care professionals who used to assume that their interests and methodologies were more disparate than similar.

This is truly a book for all those seasons—for those led apprehensive or even kicking and screaming into pastoral research as well as for those who enthusiastically indulge their curiosity in this way. It is for those who love to tinker with numbers as well as for those who look for patterns in the kind of documentation we excel at gathering—verbatims, anecdotes, case histories. It is equally useful for social workers, pastoral counselors, nurses, chaplains, pastoral educators doctoral candidates in pastoral care and counselings—all who want to do research in this area. I grabbed Larry VandeCreek's book the first time I heard the term "pastoral research" as part of my job description, and my residents and I have relied on it ever since. The reader will find equally valuable this edition, which includes comparable guidance and instructions for qualitative research from Hilary Bender and Merle Jordan.

While there will undoubtedly always be new horizons to discover and explore, I am tempted to say that this book comes just in the nick of time. Currently just coming into view are a wide array of issues to be examined, including wholistic health, homeopathic medicine, the nature and types of healing, wellness, and the impact of gender, ethnicity, cross-cultural concerns, and economics on caring and learning processes. Further, vital questions about the nature of research and the design and interplay of methodologies appropriate to our fields are being raised, particularly by those interested in what we all have to contribute to one another from our own particular disciplines. To borrow a phrase, the field is ripe for the harvest.

—Margot Hover, D.Min.

# Introduction

**R**esearch is a many-splendored thing. In its most basic and generic connotation, it is no more than systematic and scholarly inquiry. That the term carries wider and deeper meanings than this may be seen by the adjectival armada frequently attached to it: quantitative research, qualitative research, historic research, phenomenological research, evaluative research, experimental research, descriptive research, quasi-experimental research, field research, literary research, ethnographic research, etc.

The fact is, of course, that every system of inquiry created by humankind has a tradition of research and an ongoing research enterprise; and each one is supported by some sort of assumptive system or, as Giorgi (1970) has called them, "approaches." Indeed, most debates over research methods are debates over assumptions. Unfortunately, in much of traditional quantitative research, such assumptions are mostly hidden or unknown and are often not openly counted as part of the research activity itself.

The pastoral arts and sciences have not escaped this complexity of presumptions. In fact, the very nature of the pastoral arts and sciences, including that part of them called pastoral care and counseling, add a multiplicity of factors and realities which mitigate against any simple and sovereign notion of research. The fact is that the pastoral care and counseling movement has deep and nurturing roots in a variety of fields of inquiry—theology, psychology, psychiatry, scriptural studies, anthropology, ecclesiology, sociology, religious studies.

Little wonder that since its inception as a self-conscious movement, the pastoral care and counseling project has been faulted for the paucity, as well as the quality, of its research. A careful reading of that critique-oriented literature, however, cannot help but reveal that the criticisms invariably stem from a particular or a singular framework, usually the positivistic framework (Strunk, 1989). What is far more accurate, and certainly inestimably more helpful, is the realization that research in the pastoral arts and sciences has not been, and cannot be, monolithic.

The present volume does not have as its objective a detailed and comprehensive unpacking of the many assumptive systems which undergird modern research strategies and methods. Such a project would require several volumes and involve one in profound explications of such meaning-making projects as the philosophy of science, philosophical existentialism, phenomenology, and more.

Rather, this book attempts to illustrate two of the major divisions of the research landscape—the quantitative and the qualitative. Although the authors note (frequently only in passing) that these two research traditions have different histories, different methods, even different epistemologies, they do not attempt to give a full account of the relevant and very important differences between these approaches.

Instead, the authors are intent on providing the pastoral caregiver some introductory guidelines for doing research in ways appropriate to the issues the researcher wishes to address. In this regard, the volume ought to be of particular aid to advanced degree candidates whose academic and clinical programs include a research project, as well as to practitioners in the field—especially chaplains and pastoral counselors—desirous of producing factual materials which will assist them, as well as their institutions, in providing better care and more enlightened understandings of pastoral care and counseling activities.

It is also hoped that despite the fact that this volume is divided into two parts focused, respectively, on quantitative research and qualitative research, the reader will not fall into an adversarial trap by pitting one against the other. On the contrary, it is hoped that the potential researcher will see these as *different* ways of doing research, discern which way better fits the nature of the topic to be addressed, and communicate the research results in an open and honest fashion which will allow the consumer of the findings to make her or his own evaluation of the knowledge acquired.

Finally, it is hoped that this volume will encourage pastoral caregivers to consider research as an integral part of their ministry, and in so doing will not only invigorate the literature in the pastoral arts and sciences but contribute to the healing, well-being, and growth of their clients, patients, and parishioners.

# PART 1
# Quantitative Approaches

*by Larry VandeCreek*

# 1

# Why Ministers Don't Like to Do Research

S o you are interested in doing some research! Welcome to an exciting process! Oh-you are not so interested? You are reading and thinking about research because your institutional staff is pushing for research? You are reading this because you are part of a degree program which requires research? I understand. In one way of another, many of us have experienced that. At some point I too was dragged kicking and screaming into doing research. I have survived. And not only have I survived, I have actually learned to like research. I like answering the questions, uncovering the facts. If you enjoy learning how people work, you can enjoy doing research too.

My goal is to help you understand enough of science and its processes so that you can do a good job in answering your particular research questions. This increased understanding can save you anxiety, time, and effort as you make your way through the scientific process. So again I welcome you to an exciting process. I challenge you to make it interesting and eye-opening. I challenge you to learn how the research process works, how science works. This learning will put you more clearly in touch with some of the fundamental motifs of our culture and its determination to be scientific.

Perhaps you are still not sure you have the time, interest, or inclination to learn the research process. I have no quarrel with that. You have some good reasons for skepticism, fear, and doubt. The very word *research* itself can be very intimidating. It can also be confusing because the word has a variety of meanings. I will use *research* to mean systematic and intentional inquiry into a problem which produces results in the form of numbers (although other valid forms of research exist, as becomes clearly evident in Part 2 of this volume.) I also mean that findings will be made available to a professional or academic community, usually through presentation or publication. This is a difficult task.

Quantitative research is a foreign and difficult task for most ministers and they are hesitant to undertake it. I maintain that their hesitation is well-founded rather than silly or idle. It is present for very good reasons. In the remainder of this chapter, I will explore three concerns and four misconceptions about science so that you can begin to think about their influence upon you. Only then can you move ahead. I will discuss the historical relationship between science and theology, an additional reason for hesitation, in the next chapter.

## CONCERN I

When you, as a minister, begin to explore how you might conduct some research, you step into a very different world than that to which you are accustomed. In this new world, the rules are different than those which prevail in the religious community. This gives rise to the first reason for hesitation.

I want you to think back to your educational experiences in high school. In those formative years, you were finding your niche in the subject areas of greatest interest to you. Usually this niche was established as you were rewarded for good work, and this reward in turn created further interest. The increased interest generated energy. The energy generated more attention to the area of study. A reinforcement cycle was created and you began to settle into in-depth study. For some persons, this reinforcement cycle focused on mathematics, for others it was chemistry or physics. For others, however, it was history or religion or English or foreign languages. In a vague way, the students of the sciences could be distinguished from those in the humanities. At the college level, this division between the sciences and the humanities continued. As more and more focus upon your area of concentration was demanded, you moved further away from other subjects and their ways of thinking.

This process was not absolute, of course. History majors still took courses in the sciences, but probably with increasing reluctance. Chemistry majors took courses in the arts and humanities, but probably only because they were required. This process was part of a continuing struggle to find a vocational place. Many students changed majors, some even moving back and forth between the sciences and the humanities, but gradually the sorting process happened and all found a place.

Since you are now in the ministry, you probably settled into the humanities, gradually leaving the sciences behind. In so doing, you left behind not only the study of specific content such as chemistry, physics, or mathematics, but also a way of thinking about the world and what is important in it. Persons with education and interest in both the sciences and the humanities can occasionally be found, but they are exceptions.

My point is this: doing research requires you to move back toward the perspectives of the sciences and mathematics. If you liked science and mathematics in your educational work and understood something of that mentality, then moving into research may be easier for you. If you have little or no exposure to science, the research perspective will be harder to explore. In either instance, your limited exposure is probably one source of your hesitation about research. I want to facilitate that process of understanding the science and research world.

## CONCERN II

A second concern plays a role in your hesitation about doing research. This additional factor is your personality, what excites you and keeps your interest, compared to what you regard as dull, uninteresting, and mundane. Many believe that research work is the latter: dry and dull as dust. This can be true, but the real issue is more complex.

In doing research, a determining factor related to personality is the ability to be curious and to ask questions. In short, you need to venture beyond traditional, conventional ways of thinking in order to challenge assumptions and to ask new questions. Later in this book, I will discuss more extensively your need for a skeptical and critical mind as you do research. For now, you need to reflect on and search for that part of your personality which wonders if things are really the way they seem, the part which seeks to break down the whole into its parts so they can be more clearly known.

The inquiring, searching part of your personality may be difficult to find. As noted earlier, your education may not have helped you develop it. Some people also seem to possess more searching, skeptical characteristics than others. Recently, I finished a Myers-Briggs Type Indicator study of pastoral counselors in a four-state region. This instrument was chosen because other researchers have given it to thousands of people and typical characterizations of specific vocations, including parish clergy have been compiled. The results of the parish clergy studies as well as the new pastoral counselor study indicate that critical thinking typically is not the pastor's primary strength. Rather, pastors are caring, intuitive, supportive persons who emphasize need for faith and hope rather than skepticism and critical thinking (Southard, 1976). Your supportive, caring characteristics may be evident to you. You will do much better in your research work, however, if you can discover and use your critical and skeptical faculties.

How can these faculties be developed? Let me suggest a simple, straightforward methodology. Later in this book we will suggest ways in which a critical question can be developed into a research project. At the moment, my concern is to help you explore areas by asking questions.

The methodology I suggest is this. As you go about your daily routine you have contact with problems, both personal and organizational. Select problems which possess some urgency and begin to be curious about them. Having taken the first step ask: "Why is this a problem?" "What is the difficulty here?" As you explore these questions, you will begin to get behind assumptions and behaviors. This encourages exploration and searching, the foundations of research.

## CONCERN III

Like educational experience and personality, a third concern which may contribute to your hesitation about research has deep roots. Simply put, this factor is the feeling that research is not part of the clergy role, that doing science is secular and that paying attention to data, numbers, and statistical tests is contrary to the serious calling of the ministry. Ministry, you may assert, cares for the spiritual, for the soul, for God's action in the world, and for the lives of God's people. Research pays attention to none of these, it may seem to you, and involves ministers in activities quite outside their calling.

This stance toward ministry and research may be helped by openly discussing it with others. The role-binding which excludes research is only true in limited ways. For example, exegesis and hermeneutics are orderly, scientific processes involving research, although they usually do not involve mathematics. However you choose to deal with this factor, it can be a highly significant variable in making you feel uncomfortable with research.

In addition to these concerns about science and research, ministers have other reasons for hesitation concerning research. These reasons, which arise from stereotypes and misconceptions about science and research, have profound influence on us. I will conclude this chapter by discussing four of these misconceptions.

## MISCONCEPTION I:

*I must become a scientist in order to carry out research.*

A scientist is an awesome figure in our culture. The name brings with it images of persons whose theories and data have revolutionized our world. Conversely, the word may also evoke images of the "absent minded professor" who secludes himself or herself in a laboratory, far away from the realities of life. These misconceptions can either intimidate or offend us.

These images are true of few scientists, however. Most are usually quite typical of educated persons, making their livelihoods by using relevant methodologies in specific scientific areas. In many ways ministers are already scientists. Like most educated persons today, they try to think about problems and processes in a rational way, and so in a limited manner they already engage in the scientific process. The challenge to conduct a research project creates an invitation to engage in an additional technical process. This process leads to increased thoroughness and to more careful technical measurement which can in turn produce increasingly discriminating results.

If they wish to publish their work, then their studies must reflect the level of technical sophistication in the field. They will, for example, experience difficulty publishing case studies(a relatively simple scientific process) in a discipline which is already publishing quantitative measurement data. Conversely, a researcher will likely have equal difficulty publishing double blind placebo controlled studies (a highly sophisticated method) in a discipline which has not yet examined its subject matter through case studies.

You do not need to become a world-famous scientist in order to carry out respectable research. Rather you need to observe your own scientific processes and know the level of sophistication in the field you wish to study. These matters point to the next misconception.

## MISCONCEPTION II

*I must understand the scientific method to undertake research.*

This misconception is parallel to the preceding discussion. Those of us who have not majored in the sciences but remain influenced by introductory courses still often carry the fantasy that a single grand immutable method lies behind all discoveries.

Scientific process is carried out with a great diversity of methods. Competent scientific studies can be done in a variety of ways, although each must pay attention to central underlying principles. The methods of the social sciences are not those of the organic fields. A specific scientific method is always the product of the basic principles of that scientific field as they are applied to subject matter. Scientists who study human beings must respect the process of informed consent, something about which astronomers, for example, do not need to worry. Astronomers and other physical scientists, therefore, possess unique freedoms in their work. Their subject matter creates its own limitations, however. While the human sciences can directly examine, converse with, and touch their subject matter, astronomers must be content to only look at their subjects from afar and can examine only the products produced by their light. Those who study animals do not have all the constraints of working with humans, but neither can they interview their subjects or study their verbal problem solving processes. In all of these fields, scientific methods must accommodate to the subjects which are studied and this invites creativity of method.

This creativity, however, must be as true as possible to the basic principles of the scientific field. Fundamental is the need to utilize as much objectivity as possible so that findings can be defended without relying on our subjective hopes, wishes, and impressions. Methods frequently used to achieve as much objectivity as possible include the following: operational definition of terms; the use of quantitative rather than qualitative measure (hence the use of numbers); the careful recognition and control of bias and variables which influence results; the need to be skeptical, questioning, and careful in the interpretation of results; and the need to replicate studies to determine if someone else in another setting produces the same results.

## MISCONCEPTION III

*I must definitely prove my answer in order to claim credible scientific results.*

The stereotypes of science are interdependent and I hope you are gradually calling them all into question. With regard to this misconception, it is important to know that science cannot prove anything in a final way. The methodology is incapable of final proof, a fact which will be discussed further in the following chapters. At this point in the discussion, it is important to know that scientific methodologies are used to determine the likelihood that results are not simply random. Random results are useless because they are unreliable; a second identical study could produce opposite findings if the results are random. The more unusual the results, the more likely it is that they are not due to random chance. Science has qualified this in the "$p$ value." A "$p$ value" of 0.05 indicates that there is a 5% chance or less that these findings are due to random chance. A second identical study by someone else which produces equivalent results will further confirm the findings and increase confidence in the face of scientific skepticism.

Consequently, your scientific duty is to produce as competent a study as possible within the limitations of subjects, time, money, and energy, and to interpret the findings carefully. Science, technically speaking, never *proves* anything. Our call as scientists is not to offer "proof" but to produce technically competent studies which suggest conclusions and which can be replicated by others. When the conclusions reached in several studies support each other, skepticism is gradually subdued.

## MISCONCEPTION IV:

*I must endure a technical, boring, difficult process in order to complete research.*

This misconception can contain a grain of truth. The research process is a careful, technical one. Regardless of the specific methods, it uses step-by-step processes which honor underlying principles. The rest is misconception.

Yet you may say,"I never endured anything so boring or difficult as the process of doing research for my degree." It is important to note that many who say this have usually gone through the scientific process only once. And it is a miserable and difficult process for everyone the first time. Blind to the difficulties to be confronted just around the next turn, you are constantly frustrated by new problems. During this first research process, you are usually short on time, money, and patience when repeatedly confronted or challenged by faculty advisors. In the face of all this, it is easy to give up on the process, defend the results as best you can, and promise yourself never to get entangled in all this again because it is required endurance beyond your reserves.

Unfortunately, we are tempted to stop, right after having come through the worst. Having gone through the process once, you find that it becomes easier. The road map is clearer; the sense behind the process is more apparent. You can now move through the process more quickly and easily, continuing to refine your understanding. And if you are nurtured, encouraged, and guided during the first experience so that the results are exciting, then the process becomes self-perpetuating. The second, third, and forth projects further and further unravel the mystery of the problem you are studying.

That is the excitement of science and research. The facts become clearer; the undiscovered facts become a gigantic, engrossing mystery deserving of the best detective using the most sophisticated methods. Now compelled to discover the truth behind this problem, you move onward until you know the facts as clearly as possible, dispensing with fiction. Boredom is gone in that compelling rush toward the truth. The basic principles of science become second nature and the challenge is to design more and more sophisticated methods to reveal the truth as clearly as possible. The adventure of the search, the hunt, has set in and it will not let you go until you know more! Caught up in this process, you begin to reap the benefits and excitement of research.

In conclusion, further thought and reflection about these factors may make it clear why you are hesitant about quantitative research. No doubt some of the hesitation has to do with educational experience, with your personality style, with perceived conflicts regarding appropriate clergy behavior, and with various misconceptions about science. I wish to reflect further about these matters by briefly discussing the history of the relationship between religion/church and science/research in the next chapter. In that discussion, it will become clear that the church has been uncomfortable with science for centuries, and an awareness of this historical background may help you understand and overcome your hesitation.

# 2

# Struggles Between Science and Theology

The church and the clergy have struggled long and hard with their relationship to science, and consequently your hesitation concerning research possesses deep historical roots. This chapter briefly recounts the history of that relationship to help you identify the early precursors of your concerns. At the same time, the discussion should help strengthen your grasp of the history of science.

The ancient church fathers were very hesitant about science. Scientific ideas influenced their world intensely, although these ideas seem primitive now. Augustine was the first whose thoughts about science had lasting influence. He thought of scientific knowledge as spiritually barren and misleading. "Nor dost Thou draw near," he wrote, "but to the contrite in heart, nor art Thou found by the proud, no, not though by curious skill they could number the stars and the sand, and measure the starry heavens, and track the course of the planets" (Augustine, 1957, p. 66). He subsequently argued in *The Trinity* that theology must be regarded as *sapientia* (wisdom) in contrast to *scientia* (knowledge), the term he reserved for the sciences. This knowledge, he argued, was derived from transitory, temporal things and led to nothing unless it was combined with wisdom from theology. Philosophy too was a kind of science and needed the wisdom of theology (Augustine, 1963). Since philosophy was the most important science of the day, Augustine worked hard to draw it together with theology. Augustine's point of view became the foundation for theology's position as "queen of the sciences," a view which stood for centuries.

The next major change occurred in the 13th century, bringing a redefinition to the relationship. The preeminence of theology was disintegrating. The new science in the West was increasingly independent, and theology's relationship with science began to be reevaluated. As universities emerged with their scientific curricula, theology needed to demonstrate a scientific character in order to be included in the new intellectual world. This was a crucial test for theology (Pannenberg, 1976).

Thomas Aquinas defined theology as a science, thereby adjusting its Augustinian foundations. Aquinas borrowing Aristotle's model, taught that theology was a "derived science," and demonstrated its scientific character by working with the Scriptures and the Creeds. The scientific process for theology was a deductive one which drew specific theological truths out of these raw materials. Theology entered university curricula largely on the basis of Aquinas's argument (Aquinas, 1964).

Other theologians (like some today) were not convinced that theology was a science, among them Duns Scotus, Alexander of Hales, and Bonaventure. They argued that theology was a practical matter aimed at producing qualities of love and respect in human beings. Despite their argument, they were overshadowed by Aquinas and his Aristotelian arguments.

The Reformation reemphasized theology as a practical matter. Martin Luther did not see theology as a science, and, with John Calvin, he spoke strongly against the Scholastics, the theological scientists of the day. Both Luther and Calvin viewed theology as the practical study of the relationship between God and human beings. Calvin's *Institutes of the Christian Religion* was in fact the first comprehensive theology which was not grounded in Aquinas's scientific, Scholastic metaphysics of essences. Torrance claims that this charac-teristic was so distinctive that modern theology began with his work (Torrance, 1969). Be that as it may, both Luther and Calvin stood in opposition to the concept of theology as a science by virtue of their stance against the Scholastics and by virtue of their efforts to make theology more understandable to the ordinary citizen.

The interrelationship between theology and science after the Reformation was complex, in part because theological pluralism abounded, and in part because science and its influence grew rapidly. The 17th and 18th centuries were so heavily influenced by science that theologians once again began to argue that theology needed to be classified as a science if it was to maintain any intellectual respectability and influence. Friedrich Schleiermacher, for instance, defined theology as a practical science and identified it as a study of Christianity (Schleiermacher, 1966). In the subsequent decades this definition produced a number of theologies dependant upon Schleiermacher, all of which taught that a study of the history of Christianity was the heart of theology.

In 1883 Wilhelm Dilthey wrote *Einleitung in die Geisteswissenschaften*, which introduced the study of human life as scientific subject matter, and which has become a classic in the history of science (Dilthey, 1883). Ernest

Troeltsch explored theology's relationship to the human sciences as they were introduced by Dilthey. Troeltsch's early work interpreted religion as a psychological process which focused on the beautiful, the good, and the divine, all ideal contents as opposed to sensory perceptions. These, said Troeltsch, all came to expression and influence in religion and were at the core of theology's scientific study. Troeltsch's work during his life gradually moved from an individually oriented psychology of religion to a broader analysis of historical structures and their meaning. This scientific attention to meaning also became a major focus of the human sciences (Pannenberg, 1976).

With or without theology, the sciences experienced their own problems, particularly in the struggles between the human and the natural sciences. Methods used with inorganic substances could not be transposed directly into the study of humans. Experimental methods were limited and humans were not as predictable or consistent as the materials of the natural sciences. Nonetheless, the human sciences grew and gave primary attention to human interaction and meaning. H. G. Gadamer and J. Habermas argued in this regard that the human sciences were necessary as a separate group of disciplines because natural laws could not work with or characterize the presence of meaning. They suggested that human meaning was the content of the human sciences and theologians such as Troeltsch and his successors went on to suggest that this was also true of theology (Pannenberg, 1976).

The entire scientific endeavor was challenged by philosophers who came to be known as logical positivists. They argued that true science was composed of statements whose accuracy could be tested and whose truth was logically demonstrable. Early positivists, such as Carnap, argued that true propositions made assertions about reality and these assertions could be proven on the Principle of Verification. This principle essentially held that statements could be believed only after they had been scientifically tested and verified by results. He, along with others, attacked theology and allied disciplines on the basis that their propositions could not be shown to be either true or false. They charged that theology was not a science at all. Its assertions were meaningless because they did not actually describe reality in a way which could be tested or proved (Carnap, 1963).

The viewpoint of logical positivism was refined by Karl Popper. He believed that the Principle of Verification was faulty because scientific laws themselves could never be more than hypothesis. Popper pointed out that science could never claim total verification of a hypothesis because it could not possibly analyze every case of, or every situation pertinent to, the hypothesis. The hypothesis, technically speaking, remained unproven as long as a single instance of the phenomena under study remained unexamined. He declared that knowledge, therefore, should be built on the Principle of Falsification. This principle argued that, since not every instance of a problem under study could be examined, the scientist should make fair and objective selection of existing cases and test them. If no case was found which falsified the hypothesis then it could be regarded as verified, as established. Popper believed that this approach was more reasonable and would still separate true knowledge from speculation and mythology (Popper, 1963).

Popper used this argument to criticize not only theology but other sciences which had difficulty using logical methods to test and prove their conclusions. Education, psychology, and social work felt the sting of his critical analysis. These disciplines soon took steps to mimic the deductive sciences and thus defend their status. Carefully planned scientific projects which used statistical analyses began to appear in their journals.

Popper's Falsification Principle was brought to the attention of the theological community by Anthony Flew, who wrote a much-debated essay in which he concluded:

> Now it often seems to people who are not religious as if there was no conceivable event or series of events the occurrence of which would be admitted by sophisticated religious people to be sufficient reason for conceding "There wasn't a God after all" or "God does not really love us then" . . . . I therefore put . . . the simple question, "What would have to occur or to have occurred to constitute for you a disproof of the love of or existence of God?" (Flew & MacIntyre, 1955, pg. 98—99).

You can see the problem. Flew defined the methodology according to the Principle of Falsification. How could the religious community set its particular problems in this form? This was an enormous challenge. Scientists were disdainful, provocative, and proud. Sweeping claims were made. The church and theology were put on the defensive until some clarity evolved.

One part of the challenge was to determine whether the scientific approach possessed any relevance to theology at all. Did scientific methodology possess a model at all usable to theology? Many theologians tried to build a new place for theology using scientific processes as much as possible. They employed hermeneutical principles from the disciplines of history and philosophy in order to create a contemporary, defensible theological science.

Pannenberg, among others, contributed to this endeavor in *Theology and the Philosophy of Science*. He asked how theological statements could be evaluated. What kind of evidence, if any, could be used in the evaluation? For Pannenberg the emergence of these questions went hand-in-hand with the realization that scientific viewpoint had infiltrated our entire view of reality and that "the early Christian witness and the historical figure of Jesus belongs to an age which for us is past, and so their relevance to the present can be assessed only as an act of interpretation." This focus on the problem underlined the importance of hermeneutics:

> The solution of the hermeneutical problem must try to determine whether the primacy of God and his revelation over all that is human and relative . . . can, though reflection on its self-mediation in the process of Christian tradition, be stated in such a manner that, although of course it still requires faith, it does not require the possibility of basing theology on an *arbitrary* venture of faith. [emphasis added] (Pannenberg, 1976, p. 277)

Thus, hermeneutics was charged with the task of devising methods to refute the charge from positivism and the opinion common among secular society that what someone believes does not matter because all beliefs are equally valid (or invalid). Hermeneutics was to demonstrate that the content of faith was not arbitrary. In accepting this task, theology sought to build a hermeneutical methodology and a theological system which qualified as a science.

Other theologians worked at the problem in a different way. They held that while decisive falsification of theological statements was not possible, there was evidence for and against specific beliefs. Basil Mitchell presents this point of view in a remarkable parable.

> In time of war in an occupied country, a member of the resistance meets one night a Stranger who deeply impresses him. They spend that night together in conversation. The Stranger tells the partisan that he himself is on the side of the resistance—indeed that he is in command of it, and urges the partisan to have faith in him no matter what happens. The partisan is utterly convinced at that meeting of the Stranger's sincerity and constancy and undertakes to trust him. They never meet in conditions of intimacy again. But sometimes the Stranger is seen helping members of the resistance, and the partisan is grateful and says to his friends, "He is on our side." Sometimes he is seen in the uniform of the police handing over patriots to the occupying power. On these occasions his friends murmur against him; but the partisan still says, "He is on our side." He still believes that in spite of appearances the Stranger did not deceive him. Sometimes he asks the Stranger for help and receives it. Sometimes he asks and does not receive it. Then he says, "The Stranger knows best." Sometimes his friends, in exasperation say, "Well, what would he have to do for you to admit that you were wrong and that he is not on our side?" But the partisan refuses to answer. He will not consent to put the Stranger to the test. And sometimes his friends complain, "Well if that's what you mean by

his being on our side, the sooner he goes over to the other side, the
better." (Mitchell, 1955, p. 104)

This parable illustrates that evidence for and against the partisan's viewpoint
exists. The evidence is indecisive, however, because the partisan takes a faith
stance and explains the evidence in a way compatible with his faith.

This brief discussion illustrates the struggle between theology and science
for nearly two millennia. Your own concerns about the world of science may, in
fact, be part of the aftermath of these historic confrontations. In the eyes of
many religious persons, science has been the enemy, challenging the very
foundations of belief. However, fundamental changes have occurred within the
philosophy of science as positivism has begun to crumble, and these changes
merit attention. The new philosophies of science are more moderate and more
compatible with the tasks of the life sciences and theology. You may find the
contributions of Michael Polanyi and Thomas Kuhn helpful.

As early as 1946 Polanyi was insisting that science was highly diverse and
not created by a simple rationalistic process as the positivists had supposed. He
argued that the intuition, presuppositions, and faith of the scientist are fundamental to discovery. He pointed out that science needs to be understood as a
community of inquirers held together by a common faith. This faith is not in
the exercise of the scientific method, but rather in a discipline imposed by scientists upon themselves in the interest of discovering an objective, impersonal
truth. The essence of this faith is that such truth exists and can be found by
disciplined research and study. This faith is fundamental, intertwined with the
entire scientific milieu of the culture, and can be defended only by further
statement of the scientist's faith. Polanyi insists that "we have no clear conception of how discovery comes about," noting that "either you know what you
are looking for, and then there is no problem; or you do not know what you are
looking for, and then you are not looking for anything and cannot expect to
find anything" (Polanyi, 1964).

This dilemma has not been as powerful for him as its initial impact would
imply because he acknowledges a creative rhythm in scientific work. His
description may apply to your own experience:

> In the course of any single experimental inquiry the mutual stimulus
> between intuition and observation goes on all the time and takes on
> the most varied forms. Most of the time is spent in fruitless efforts,
> sustained by a fascination which will take beating after beating for
> months on end, and produce ever new outbursts of hope, each as
> fresh as the last so bitterly crushed the week or month before.
> Vague shapes of the surmised truth suddenly take on the sharp
> outlines of certainty, only to dissolve again in the light of second

thoughts or of further experimental observations. Yet from time to time, certain visions of the truth, having made their appearance, continue to gain strength both by further reflection and additional evidence. These are the claims which may be accepted as final by the investigator and for which he may assume public responsibility by communicating them in print. (Polanyi, 1964, p. 30)

In a later work Polanyi develops this philosophy of science further. He states that the "complete objectivity as usually attributed to the exact sciences is a delusion and is in fact a false ideal." In its place he offers the concept of "personal knowledge" which explores the dimensions of doubt and commitment in scientific endeavors. This personal knowledge involves "a coherent system of superior knowledge, upheld by people mutually recognizing each other as scientists, and acknowledged by modern society as its guide." Thus, he concludes that this superior knowledge includes "all that is coherently believed to be right and excellent by men within their culture" (Polanyi, 1985).

Polanyi's description of the scientific process, indeed his definition of science itself, is very different from the positivists. To him, science is an interpretive process, a process of providing a framework for facts rather than a process which verifies or falsifies statements. The framework itself is based on assumptions accepted *a priori*.

Polanyi's point of view is not new. He reiterates an older point of view which was never completely submerged during the era of positivists. Francis Peabody wrote about medicine during the heyday of the positivists. His famous essay "The Care of the Patient" is a classic statement of that point of view:

It is rather fashionable to say that the modern physics has become too scientific. [Was the care of this patient] . . . too scientific or was it not scientific enough? The popular conception of a scientist as a man who works in a laboratory and who uses instruments of precision is as inaccurate as it is superficial, for a scientist is known, not by his technical processes but by his intellectual processes; and the essence of the scientific method of thought is that it proceeds in an orderly manner toward the establishment of truth. (Peabody, 1927, p. 879)

Thomas Kuhn's viewpoint is rooted in a historical perspective and is compatible with Polanyi's. Kuhn argues that a limited number of world-shaking scientific revolutions have taken place and that each revolution has introduced a new paradigm, a new way of thinking. Each new paradigm completely restructures a particular field of science and, once it is widely accepted, suggests the questions which demanded further research. This further research creates a "normal science" which says Kuhn, is "a mopping up operation . . . [which]

engages most scientists throughout their careers." This "normal science" is further described by Kuhn as paradigm-dependent (Kuhn, 1970).

Kuhn's philosophy posits that, in the course of time, this paradigm-dependent research not only turns up data which explains and elucidates the paradigm, but also data which challenges the paradigm. In this way, the limitations of the paradigm become more evident until finally it is so weakened that a new structure is suggested which accounts for data in a more creative and exciting way. An historical example will make his concept clearer:

> Today's physics textbooks tell the student that light is photons, i.e, quantum-mechanical entities that exhibit some characteristics of waves and some particles. Research proceeds accordingly, or rather according to the more elaborate and mathematical characterization from which this usual verbalization is derived. That characterization of light is, however, scarcely half a century old. Before it was developed by Planck, Einstien, and others early in this century, taught that light was transverse wave motion, a conception rooted in a paradigm that derived ultimately from the optical writings of Young and Fresnel in the early nineteenth century. Nor was the wave theory the first to be embraced by almost all practitioners of optical science. During the eighteenth century the paradigm for this field was provided by Newton's *Opticks*, which taught that light was material corpuscles. At that time physicists sought evidence, as the early wave theorists had not, of the pressure exerted by light particles impinging on solid bodies. These transformations of the paradigms of physical optics are scientific revolutions, and the successive transition from one paradigm to another via revolution is the usual developmental pattern of mature science. (Kuhn, 1970, pp. 11–12)

Kuhn also believes that this movement from paradigm to paradigm is not a cumulative acquisition of knowledge which leads to a better and better "fit" between nature and knowledge. Science, according to Kuhn, does not progress. He points out that it is not intrinsically better to believe that light is photons rather than transverse wave motion. Rather, he suggests, the contemporary theory explains current facts as we know them and fits our common sense about the world. And the genius of the scientist, he said, is expressed in the ability to see the facts in a new light. The genius of Antoine Lavoisier, who discovered oxygen, was that he "saw oxygen where Priestly had seen dephlogisticated air and where others had seen nothing at all" (Kuhn, 1970, p. 118).

Another example from Kuhn illustrates that the essence of science is the ability to see the world in a new way, and thus it is a highly subjective process:

> Since remote antiquity most people have seen one or another heavy body swinging back and forth on a string or chain until it finally

comes to rest. To the Aristotelians, who believed that a heavy body is moved by its own nature from a higher position to a state of natural rest at a lower one, the swinging body was simply falling with difficulty, constrained by the chain, tortuous motion and a considerable time. Galileo, on the other hand, looking at the swinging body, saw a pendulum, a body that almost succeeded in repeating the same motion over and over again *ad infinitum*. And having seen that much, Galileo observed other properties of the pendulum as well and constructed many of the most significant and original parts of his new dynamics around them . . . All of these natural phenomena he saw differently from the way they had been seen before. (Kuhn, 1970, pp. 118–119)

Kuhn believes that the faith of the scientist plays a key role in these paradigm changes. Paradigms are not subject to proof and are highly prized by the adherents in part, of course, because most of their work is paradigm dependent. Changes in scientific points of view, therefore, come about through long years of struggle. He repeats Max Planck's comment that "new scientific truth does not triumph by convincing its opponents and making them see the light, but rather because its opponents eventually die and a new generation grows up that is familiar with it."

This chapter has reviewed the historical relationship between theology and science, noted theology's attempt to shape itself into a science, and concluded with a summary of two contemporary philosophies of science. These contemporary perspectives move away from the rigid narrowness of positivism and view science as a broad social and intellectual phenomenon based upon many assumptions about the world. The scientist seeks to be objective within the confines of these assumptions. This perspective is more compatible with pastoral care and counseling and may be more encouraging to you. If you find yourself continuing to think about science as proving the truth in an absolute way, then remember the perspectives of Polanyi and Kuhn. Science is composed of a community of scholars who ask you to join with them in answering questions by using accepted, disciplined methodologies.

# 3

# Moving Ahead:
# Concerns at the Beginning

**W**e need to push forward, beyond the issues of hesitation and history. This chapter will discuss the fundamental ingredients and attitudes which shape quantitative research work. The discussion is divided into three parts: 1) the ways in which you are already scientific, 2) assumptions of the scientific researcher, and 3) research pitfalls.

## YOU ARE ALREADY SCIENTIFIC

Research work requires a scientific process and this realization can be frightening. "What do I know about the scientific process?" you ask. Being scientific is not as strange as it seems, however. You are already scientific simply by your participation in Western culture even though you may not have conducted research projects. Scientific attitudes are so much a part of the fabric of your culture that you scarcely recognize them. How can you become aware of this fundamental scientific stance?

Imagine yourself living in an illiterate, prescientific culture. Such a culture could be found in ancient history or in a current primitive tribe. In this culture neither reading nor writing would exist. Knowledge would consist of what was remembered from generation to generation. It would be as fragile as life itself because if the only "knower" died, then the knowledge would disappear. Books would not be available; no dictionaries or libraries would exist. Much energy would be devoted to day-to-day survival and to remembering the available knowledge.

As Walter J. Ong (1982) has pointed out, the memory process would rely upon thinking memorable thoughts. This would be accomplished by creating mnemonic patters involving highly rhythmical, patterned language dominated by verbal formulas and memorable sayings. This language process would encourage memory at the expense of exact details, and attention to clear, accurate factual observation would be minimal. "Objectivity would not be valued because," as Ong has noted, "knowing means achieving close, empathic, communal identification with the known. Knowing means getting into and with that which is rather than the objectivity we scientific persons have come to assume." And, since meaning and interpretation are understood in this way, the facts and events would be edited and rearranged to ease the burden of memory and to promote the perceived meaning. If you imagine yourself in such a culture, you realize that science would be practically impossible. You also realize how implicitly scientific you are.

The development from a prescientific into a scientific culture required centuries of struggle. The essence of this process was the development of the ability to distinguish between subjective impression and objective observation, a cornerstone of science. Two illustrations will make clear that this development occurred much later in human history than is often assumed.

The first illustration arises from St. Luke's management of historical materials as he wrote his Gospel and the Acts. Many scholars agree that Luke, as a physician (thus scientist) and historian of his day, created some problems for us in his management of materials. Various difficulties exist and these are described in standard critical New Testament studies. Many of these difficulties, however, are rooted in St. Luke's emphasis upon meaning rather than factuality. He did not distinctly separate facts and meanings. Nor could we expect him to do this because this distinction had not yet been clearly developed. Martin Dibelius comments on these phenomena:

> The ancient historian does not wish to present life with photographic accuracy, but rather to portray and illuminate what is typical, and his practice of aiming at what is typical and important allows the author of Acts partly to omit, change, or generalize what really occurred. So it is that, where he sometimes appears to us today to be idealizing and describing what was typical, he was really trying to discharge his obligation as a historian (Dibielius, 1956, pp. 136-37).

If you find this perspective ridiculous or unique, it is a measure of how scientific you have yourself become, all the while forgetting that this scientific mentality is very new in the history of humanity. The historian's task in the New Testament period was not first of all to put down a chronological sequence of events. St. Luke wrote, indeed, that he was setting forth "an orderly account" but this seems to refer not so much to a factual and chronological order as we think of it today as to a meaningful logical or even theological order. Principles of scientific objectivity had not yet been developed.

A second example is even closer to modernity. Once again, the careful reporting of observed events will be missing and your response to this will demonstrate how scientific you are. The 14th century Black Plague which swept through Europe arrived in Sicily late in 1347, carried by infected sailors from seaport to seaport. Once it was discovered in a city, the citizens would make valiant efforts to combat the disease. Their usual choice of intervention was to parade religious relics in the streets while reciting litanies, hoping by this means to drive away the evil spirits who brought the disease. This was itself an unscientific process, but that is not the point of interest here. Rather, a historian of that period recounted the procession of priest and people in Messina, Sicily, carrying with them holy water and the relics of St. Agatha. The historian's narrative of the events on that day notes that

> while the whole population was thus processing around the streets, a black dog, bearing a drawn sword in his paws, appeared among them, gnashing with its teeth and rushing upon and breaking all the silver vessels and lamps and candlesticks on the altars, and casting them hither and thither . . . (Zeigler, 1969, p. 41)

The factuality of this statement, written by Michael of Piazza in approximately 1360, is doubtful. Today, most will doubt that a black dog appeared carrying a drawn sword in his front paws while walking on his two rear legs. Most will doubt that because they have never seen it happen, but even more so because it contradicts contemporary expectations concerning dogs. The important point, however, is that Michael of Piazza did not seem to be concerned about such an unscientific, erroneous observation in 1360. He appears not to be concerned with the possibility that others would laugh at and dismiss his account as ridiculous. Indeed, he did not need to be concerned about this because the need for critical, accurate observation had not been established even then. As in the previous example, the author was so interested in making a point, in rendering an interpretation of the tragic and lethal plague that he reversed fact and interpretation by placing meaning before accurate observation of events. Many additional examples could be cited, examples in the 20th century.

How strange this inversion of fact and interpretation seems. Today it is very clear that the facts come first. "Get the facts straight," you say, "and then interpret them." Such an attitude is a demonstration that you are deeply scientific, that the foundations for understanding research are already present.

In conclusion, you are more scientific than you realize. The foundations are in place even though you may not have completed college science courses or cultivated a skeptical, critical attitude in your professional work. You know that facts need to be observed and data collected before you begin interpretation. You know that assumptions and biases are important because you can easily see your results the way you want to see them, neglecting obvious alternate interpretations. You know all that and more as a product of growing up in a scientific culture. With these basics in place, you can adopt the additional assumptions necessary for scientific activity.

## ASSUMPTIONS OF THE SCIENTIFIC RESEARCHER

The aim of the previous section was to demonstrate that you are more scientific than you first thought. You realize that careful observation precedes interpretation. Conducting your own research project builds upon that realization. This section will expand your basic awareness to include three assumptions which are fundamental to the research process. Many others exist because the research perspective is an integrated world view. These assumptions, however, are basic and hopefully will encourage you to explore further details of the research process.

ASSUMPTION I:
*The world and human experience are more complicated than they appear*

This fundamental assumption of science is widely accepted in our culture. Today we assume that the world and life possess a "depth" which does not meet the eye, which is not immediately apparent. The scientific process digs into this depth so as to discover more about it. Telescopes look outward into space and microscopes look inward into the smallest elements of matter. Life experiences are examined by psychotherapy as well as the social and behavioral sciences.

The assumption that the world and experience contain "depth" is, in itself, not a unique assumption of science. Ancient prescientific cultures all assumed a depth complicatedness to reality. Gods and demons were behind every event, present in every hill and tree, and constantly active. Their understanding of this depth, like ours, controlled and directed much of life.

The scientific mentality responds to this depth in its own unique way because research seeks to take everything apart. Conventional research methodologies ensure careful work and reliable evidence upon which to base conclusions. Adherence to these scientific rules and methods is the scientific process.

Fundamental issues between theology and science arise at this juncture. Both religion and science seek to find and describe the truth concerning this depth. Many have argued that these two are enemies, partly because their methods and assumptions differ, but this argument is an oversimplification. In the past, religion shared the methods of the prescientific world. As discussed in chapter 2, religion had its struggles with science as it developed, but parallel struggles were taking place in other fields as they opposed science. The struggle between religion and science has been particularly difficult because both deal with basic assumptions about life and its meaning. In the adjustment process, theology increasingly realized the potential benefits to be gained by more interest in science.

In this adjustment process, theology has also become aware that science is limited by its very methods. Science cannot study, at least in mathematical terms, many of the most important elements of personal life, although this is contested by many enthusiasts of science. Consider the following example from personal life.

A scientist returns home from work. This man is a hardcore scientist, let's say a physicist or a molecular biologist, even a mechanical engineer. He makes his living by applying scientific principles and he believes strongly in scientific methodologies. He might be tempted to believe that every important part of life can be analyzed by science. On this particular day he hears his three-year-old daughter crying as he enters the house and he is momentarily worried. Some severe viral infections have attacked neighborhood children and he hopes his daughter is not among them. He moves through the house straight to where his daughter is crying and finds to his relief that her tears originate in a minor concern. He sits down and plays with her for a while, unaware of how scared he had momentarily become and how relived he now feels.

This story illustrates a simple but core human experience. But how can science study it? How can it study his parental concern for his daughter, his momentary worry, and his sense of relief? Objective data cannot be obtained. Perhaps some self-reported measures can be taken of their impact, but these will be at best difficult to obtain and to compare with the experiences of others.

What conclusions can be drawn from this? The church and theology can derive great benefits from attention to scientific study. They cannot blindly ignore science, giving blanket endorsement to everything religious, past and present. Conversely, the church and theology should not worship scientific methods. These methods can study the larger and smaller world, but cannot detect, measure, or analyze many of the deeper facets of life, the very facets which are at the core of theology. Scientists may devote their professional lives to scientific activity, but their own personal lives will be carried along by assumptions and meanings which can never be tested. These assumptions and meanings posses a religious character because they refer to ultimate foundations and the very character of the world and life. In this way, religion and science are complementary, needing and benefiting from each other.

You can make a contribution to science by the way you put the world together as a theologian and by the way you take it apart as a scientific person and as a scientist. Taking the world apart requires a basic attitude and leads to the second assumption.

ASSUMPTION II:
*A skeptical, critical, questioning viewpoint is necessary concerning this "depth" and leads to increased objectivity.*

This second assumption contains two elements: the importance of skepticism and the necessity of objectivity. The depth within the world and life is best exposed through a skeptical, critical, questioning stance which then creates objectivity.

Concerning the first element, science assumes that the world and life do not automatically reveal their depth. In fact, a camouflage hides their true character. A skeptical, critical, questioning attitude is required in order to strip away this outer layer of appearances and to discover the truth.

This thoroughgoing, persistent skepticism may seem strange and new to you. Ministers are taught to exercise acceptance, faith, and belief; science requires doubt and constant questioning. Assumptions in the two fields are reversed.

The purpose of this questioning is to produce objectivity, the cornerstone of science. This is the second element of the assumption. Attaining objectivity requires that you test subjective, vested interests as well as first impressions, becoming aware of biases and erroneous assumptions about your subject matter. Objectivity requires the courage and skill to "see things as they are" rather than the way you would like them to be.

Objectivity is always relative, of course. True, complete objectivity is never possible for the human being. You must always stand somewhere in your own subjective world—you must always assume something. You will always to a certain extent "see through a glass darkly." This incomplete and elusive quality of objectivity does not argue against its role in your work, however. You will never be completely objective, but neither are you completely truthful, honest, caring, loving, dependable, understanding, or respectful. These present challenges. In science, the achievement of objectivity is the challenge composed of reducing bias and resisting the temptation to "jump to conclusions." The rigorous methods of science are directed towards this goal.

As you develop your research work, apply this objectivity first of all to your assumptions about your subject matter. What do you already accept as fact?

What are the "hard facts" already produced by solid studies? This concern demonstrates the importance of reading reports of previous studies. Such reading encourages you to grapple with the finding of other researchers and to examine their assumptions. The evidence generated by a study is only as good as the accuracy of the assumptions. If you disagree with a previous researcher's assumptions, the evidence and conclusions will not likely be acceptable because a direct relationship exists between what you assume and what you "discover." When you disagree with another's assumptions, you need to develop and defend your own, thereby running the risk of criticism. Such personal initiative, however, also creates a unique opportunity for new discovery.

Skeptical thinking must be applied secondly to the research methodology you develop for your study. As will be discussed further in later chapters, a methodology is strongest when it generates data through a variety of deliberately formed groups and under controlled situations. Research is strong when skepticism cannot discredit the results.

The application of sufficient skepticism to your assumptions and methodology comprises a difficult task. The difficulty lies chiefly in blindness to the process. Charging ahead into data gathering and analysis, the results strip away the blindness when they are confused or meaningless. But then it is too late. The data gathering is completed and the project cannot be salvaged.

A personal experience will illustrate the importance of objectivity and skeptical thinking. Twenty years ago the administration of an inner-city neighborhood health center sought data from the community concerning the need for expanded services. Forms were constructed and staff members recruited to gather data through personal contacts and interviews. The results were initially confusing because each investigator's data differed. A skeptical review soon revealed, however, that the data from each staff member supported the need for expanded services in his or her particular professional area. Data gathered by physicians documented the need for more medical services; chaplaincy data called for more religious and pastoral counseling services. The list was as long as the professional diversity of the interviewers. The administration threw out the study results. They were useless.

No doubt many factors contributed to this interesting phenomenon. Major problems existed in the foundational assumptions of the study and its methodology. The planners assumed, probably for financial reasons, that the staff members could collect objective data from personal interviews. The planners assumed that an inner-city resident, knowing the professional affiliation of the interviewer, could provide accurate data in a personal interview. However, the results suggest that respondents gave what they believed would be interviewer-approved responses. The planners assumed that staff members could rise above

their own territorial concerns and be objective. The results suggest that interviewers contributed to confusing data. Sufficient skepticism was not exercised
and objectivity was minuscule.

ASSUMPTION III:
*Science protects and promotes objectivity by emphasizing the need for discussion with
and review by experienced research peers.*

This assumption emphasizes that research cannot be a solitary individual-
ized experience, devoid of peer contact. New researchers usually try to
established a wall of privacy and isolation around their work, rationalizing that
criticism is unfair or that their ideas may be stolen. In reality, they are usually
struggling with their insecurity and feelings of vulnerability as researchers.
They may even recount stories of Galileo, Pasteur, and other early researchers
who worked alone. Such days are gone; research is now a communal effort. As
a result, most funding agencies will not provide grant money to individuals in
their own names, and all research within institutions, from established professionals as well as students, is peer reviewed. In some settings where mistakes
may be life-threatening, peer reviewers may require investigators to make
specific changes in design before they can proceed.

Such communal supervision is not mere bureaucratic intrusion. In performing research, you join colleagues who are devoted to the discovery of facts
which clarify the nature of the world and life. This is a disciplined as well as
difficult process and collegial review is in reality an essential means of
promoting appropriate skepticism and objectivity.

If you are new to research work, some type of consultation or supervision is
essential. Ask yourself serious questions when your reluctance and resistance to
such contact emerges. Let experienced colleagues help you. No one expects you
to have all the answers about your design. No one expects you to be perfect.
Put aside your pride as well as fear and explore your ideas with experienced
colleagues.

## RESEARCH PITFALLS LEADING TO UNFINISHED WORK.

By now it is clear that a research project requires a careful, disciplined
process. If you are conducting your first project, you can legitimately expect
some problems. Unfortunately, these difficulties sometimes overwhelm the new
researcher.

A pastoral counselor tells a story about the screening interview conducted
by a graduate program to which he had applied. The program director, having
welcomed him, showed him a drawer of student files, one-fourth of which were

marked "completed." He added that the remaining three-fourths of the students, having finished the course work, never completed the research. The basic pitfall in research work is the inability to finish the project. While work completion is necessary to acquire gratification and reward, no research is worth the effort if it cannot be finished. Five principal factors contribute to unfinished research.

### Diminished Motivation

The lack of motivation to continue with the chosen research area is a major factor. What area do you wish to study? Is it pastoral counselor management of depression, minister malpractice, parish minister satisfaction, pastoral care financial productivity in the hospital, or the effects of sermons? Whatever your chosen area, you must be deeply motivated because only this will carry you through the entire process. A passing superficial curiosity is insufficient. This accounts for much unfinished research. Difficulties outstrip interests and the entire process falters.

Careful thought and self-examination are required when choosing a research area within which to work. Two suggestions are in order. First give the selection process some time to mature. Do not make the decision on a day or a week. Ask yourself if your current interest area leads to a deeper, even more fundamental interest. If so, move to the exploration of this deeper interest.

Second, discuss your ideas with colleagues, friends, and advisors. Let them help you with the selection process. You do not need all the answers before raising your interests for discussion. Let them explore new and diverse aspects of your interest. Assume that you can sort out the confusion they create and be the better for it.

### An Unrealistic Timetable

A second factor which leads to incomplete work is the failure to set a timetable, at least one which can be realistically met. Some persons begin research with no timetable at all. This simply does not work because every day duties constantly claim priority. Additionally, few remain interested in the same subject forever or have unlimited time and energy. The research must be completed while your interest lasts. Maintaining this timetable requires personal discipline, the same kind of discipline required by the entire scientific process.

You may suffer from the opposite problem. You may set timetables which are unreasonably short and lead to endless frustration. Such a timetable leaves no room for sorting through confusion and working out problems and delays. Self-knowledge and a realistic look at the work schedule are essential here.

*Excessively High Expectations of Impact*

A third factor which leads to incomplete work occurs when your positive expectations about the impact of the results are not met. Research work seeks to produce important knowledge. Such knowledge should have impact on the problem. But this expectation becomes a trap when your fantasies about the real and immediate difference your research will create are dashed. Be particularly alert if these fantasies seek to prove a point or create a change in persons or institutions. Your single research project will seldom result in such change. The persons or organizations may at best receive your results with interest and ignore their implications. The history of science contains many examples of ignored research results. This lack of recognition leads to researcher burnout if the motivation for the work was to produce a high impact on selected individuals, churches, denominations, hospitals, or counseling centers.

*Excessive Vested Interest In The Results*

A fourth factor which leads to incomplete work and frustration is research in which you possess vested interest and high stakes in the outcome, stakes so high that you cannot possibly be objective. Suppose you are a chaplain at a health care institution and, when confronted with some administrative skepticism about your contribution to patient care, you decide to conduct a research project. You decide to gather data from patients and staff to answer the skepticism. This motivation itself creates a major problem. You have a vested interest in securing positive results. Suppose the project produces such results. You are now relieved. You have solved the problem because you can now demonstrate a contribution to patient care. But you will be surprised. Who will believe the results? Closet skeptics will emerge everywhere. They will doubt the results just because you benefitted by them. They will suspect that you lacked the proper objectivity and have indulged in self-promotion.

This vested interest in research can result in more complications still. Let us suppose that the results suggest that the chaplain makes no contribution. Your expectations have not been met. You have generated results which are professionally damaging to yourself. The administration will believe the results because they confirm their initial impression. The research will not be rewarded. You may, in fact, lose your job, and the results may be passed around the country by your administrator. Then other chaplains will become upset and angry at you. Isolated in the proverbial doghouse, you will be professionally punished without realizing your expectations.

From this point of view, you should always ask what could be the worst possible outcome of your research. You should avoid projects in which you are not ready for the worst possible outcome. In this instance, your fantasies concerning the positive impact of your work come crashing down in disappointment as you realize that you have created a no-win situation. In frustration you will be tempted to throw up your hands and give up on research. In reality, the problem lies with selecting a research area in which you possessed excessively high expectations and a vested interest in specific results.

Thus, to return to the original theme, the ability to complete the work is related to the choice of a research area. Your research area needs to be one in which you are deeply interested. Yet you need to avoid those areas where others would suspect that you are naturally biased and less than objective. And, practically speaking, do not undertake projects unless you are ready for the worst possible outcome.

## Problems With Practical Details

A fifth factor which leads to incomplete research consists of problems with practical details. These problems are inherent in your circumstances, both personal and professional. Some of them, however, are created by not thinking through the project in concrete fashion during the planning stage. One example of this problem occurs over and over and is worth special mention.

As you plan your project, ask whether you can get the raw data for your project. Do you have access to the people whom you need as subjects? What stands between you and your subjects? Whose permission will you need? Failure to clarify this issue will result in creation of a splendid project which cannot be completed. Suppose you want to gather survey data concerning the fear of death in seminary and medical students, comparing the two groups. Although a worthy subject, the important detail is whether you will have contact with these groups. If not, data gathering will be a nightmare. Seminary and medical deans stand between you and the students. Their respective institutions will have policies which govern access to their students. Even if approval is obtained, only a limited number of busy seminary and medical students will likely respond to a questionnaire. Response rate then becomes a problem, manifest, of course, only after you have invested so much in the project that changes cannot be made.

Other practical problems exist. Many are unique to specific projects. Most can be spotted when you concretely outline the project step-by-stp. Make a detailed list of contacts and actions your project requires. Then talk this over with your colleagues and consultant. What is their experience? Where do they see problems? Constantly ask yourself where complications could arise. This process will greatly increase the likelihood that you can finish the work.

In summary, you are more scientific than you realize. This scientific sense forms a base upon which you can build. This building can take place by paying careful attention to the fundamental assumptions of the scientific process. This disciplined process contains many pitfalls which can result in incomplete work. These pitfalls include insufficient motivation for the project, the lack of an appropriate time schedule, excessive vested interest in specific results, and difficulty in managing practical problems.

How then can you proceed? Perhaps it all seems impossible. You would like to do some research, but it now seems to you that the areas in which you are motivated are also those in which you are too invested to be objective. Perhaps it seems that the worst possible outcome precludes the exploration of those areas in which you are really interested. Perhaps research just seems too complicated.

If these are your sentiments, I am encouraged. Your chances of completing the project have increased. Shortly we will be discussing the technical processes of doing research. These processes, while they may seem strange to you, are cognitive and less subtle than the preceding discussion. If you have appreciated the difficulties discussed, then you have taken a giant step.

# 4

# Creating the Question

Research, as an answering process, seeks responses to specific questions. As researcher, you develop these questions to narrow your interest area into a manageable study. In empirical research (as described in this book) the questions narrow the subject matter even further because quantitative answers are required. This chapter describes selected facets of this process and then develops an example. Finally, the process by which research questions lead to hypotheses will be discussed.

Science begins its disciplined process by creating research questions. Standing at the head of the scientific process, these questions have a lasting impact upon the project. The roots of research confusion and difficulty later in the project are usually hidden within inadequately defined research questions. This technical process challenges you to move with increasing clarity from a general research interest area to specific research questions and to clarify over and over again exactly what you want to know. This clarification process requires patience and skill over weeks and months of work.

During this clarification process, at least two temptations confront you. The first consists of refusal to engage in the clarification and narrowing process at all. Giving in to this temptation, you simply engage in a research "fishing expedition," gathering little bits of data here and there in a variety of forms and shapes. You exercise little, if any, control, and the methodology produces a hodgepodge of information which cannot be interpreted in a meaningful way. As a novice researcher, you may be gravely tempted toward this "anything goes" approach, often a product of research inexperience. Futile attempts to publish the results usually produce a cure for this temptation. More discipline is needed in order to manage the process, control the variables, and avoid being overwhelmed and confused.

The second temptation invites you to formulate the questions prematurely. This temptation involves grasping any questions which occur to you and making them the focus of study. You avoid the struggle of working through the confusion. This temptation appeals to researchers who believe that any research question is good enough, to those who have procrastinated so long that questions must be developed in a few days, and to all who lack the patience or ability to tolerate and clarify the confusion involved in solidifying a study. This hasty process bears bitter fruit months later as interest lags, doubts overcome energy, and the specter of an unfinished project begins to loom ahead. Avoiding either of these temptations commits you to fight your way into clarity, asking over and over again, "What are my questions? What do I want to know?"

This clarification process will best proceed through conversation with others about your ideas and your confusions. Consulting knowledgeable research colleagues is mandatory here. No one can work through the "mud of confusion" without others who will listen and provide feedback. Most degree programs mandate such consultation with advisors as well as fellow students, and experienced researchers continue to rely upon it.

Reading the literature permits unknown colleagues to be your consultants. These authors describe their questions and how they studied them. They will often raise additional questions for study at the end of their report. And do not forget the skepticism of science—one project by itself is relatively weak. Additional studies by yourself or others are always more convincing. These additional studies confirm the validity of the first study, or, in fact, raise new questions about it.

How can you find this literature? No substitute exists for a good library and librarian. You can start by looking for books, but journals will likely be your best source. Your subject may lend itself to a computerized search of indexed journals. Other references include *Dissertation Abstracts International (DAI)*, *Psychological Abstracts*, *Sociological Abstracts*, and Educational Resources Information Center (ERIC). *Religious and Theological Abstracts* is published four times per year and *Abstracts of Research in Pastoral Care and Counseling* is published annually. Search these and other abstracting publications or bibliographies for important references. This entire process produces some clearer awareness of what you want to study.

Thus, creating research questions demands clear, disciplined thinking which rests on the ability to both tolerate confusion and to clarify, clarify, and clarify again. No substitute exists for carefully exploring every facet related to your potential project. These explorations take you in many directions at once, raise many potential research questions, and further refine your thinking. Clear, disciplined thinking gradually helps you clarify all this confusion into one set of questions which epitomizes your interests. This process will become clearer as we develop the illustration begun in the previous chapter.

## AN EXAMPLE

In the last chapter, I discussed a research effort devoted to discovering the effects of chaplains upon hospital patients. Let us suppose that, having weighed the risks, you decide to proceed. Now you need to shape this interest into a manageable research question. I will develop only a single question here for the sake of simplicity, but many projects develop multiple, parallel, and related questions.

How can this question be developed? Immediately, an additional concern intrudes, a concern not about developing the question, but about research design. Development of the question and the research design go hand-in-hand even though we are discussing them in separate chapters here. The research question always implies a design, and as you develop the question you need to know two things about research designs. First, a design always implies such practical details as budget, time, space, energy, and skill. You will see how this happens as we develop this research question, and I will discuss it more fully in a later chapter. The second thing you need to know about research designs is that they are ranked according to their power, their capacity to produce convincing data in the face of skepticism. A single case study, for example, is less powerful than data gathered from 100 subjects.

This design concept is important at this moment because you may wish to construct a two-group comparison study. Suppose you wish to compare the effects of pastoral care provided by chaplains to the effects of pastoral care provided by parish pastors who visit at the hospital. This requires a two-group design and its power rests with the capability to compare the two groups. You could argue that the pastoral care effectiveness of parish pastors forms a baseline against which chaplaincy work could be measured.

After thinking about this possibility periodically for a few days, you realize that this comparison also poses problems. What would the parish pastors think? Would they think you were trying to make them look bad? If you told them about the project, would they immediately try to do better visitations, thereby introducing a temporary, artificial variable? Would they feel in competition with you, that is, that the project would create a winner and a loser?

Additionally, who would collect trustworthy data from patients? Would patients likely tell you the whole truth about these two relationships? You would need to find a way to gather "objective" data. Another potential problem would be that patients could seek to protect their pastors and rank them higher just because they know them and have to return to that religious community. Here another variable emerges. Perhaps this comparison needs to take into account whether the patient likes or dislikes the pastor. Maybe the patient would rank the chaplain higher just because he or she does not like the pastor. But then there is another variable. Maybe the patient's ranking would have a relationship to the type of illness. Perhaps illnesses with social stigmas or highly personal qualities permit more help from the chaplain because the patient wants to keep the pastor out of such highly personal matters. And what about the gender of the chaplain and the patient? That too is likely to be influential. Suppose the study examined the effectiveness of pastoral care from a male parish pastor and a female chaplain.

The possibility of a comparison study generates these as well as other concerns. They do not prohibit the project but an awareness of their presence and influence means that you can take them into account during your further thinking. You must somehow contend with them because you are identifying variables which impact upon the data and your management of them must be described and defended in your report. The motivation to work them out lies in the need to create as powerful, as convincing a study as possible.

Let us suppose that, after thinking it over, you set aside the possibility of a comparison study involving chaplains and parish pastors. The problems seem too great. You will simply study the effects of chaplains on hospital patients, though a comparison design using chaplains is still possible.

How can this interest area be narrowed? Take the nouns of the phrase, "the effects of chaplains upon hospital patients," and ask as many questions about them as possible. Consider the three nouns and their modifiers one at a time.

"Chaplains"
  What chaplains?
  - Chaplains only at your institution? What about chaplains at other institutions?
  - If others are included, will these chaplains be from both general and psychiatric hospitals?
  - Will only staff chaplains be involved? What about chaplains in training?
  - Will the staff chaplains involved include only those who have certified training in hospital ministry?
  - Will Protestant, Catholic, and Jewish chaplains be involved?
  - Will chaplains include only selected Protestant denominations?
  - Will the study include both male and female chaplains?

- Will chaplains be included or excluded because of age or length of experience?

"Hospital Patients"

What hospital patients?
- Both male and female patients?
- Both patients with and without church membership?
- Patients regardless of which physician admitted them?
- Emergency room patients who are never admitted to the hospital?
- Healthy mothers and their new babies?
- Patients regardless of diagnoses?
- Only those patients who had at least an initial visit from the chaplain?
- Patients irrespective of the amount of time the chaplain spent with them?
- Patients who live outside the city or county?
- Will data be gathered from family members? If so, which family members would be involved?

These questions raise many new issues, some of which permit a comparison study. Should the project involve more than one institution? Who, as regards chaplains and patients, will be included and excluded from the project? Where will you draw the line? At this stage, research is a process of "drawing the line," of defining and redefining who is included and excluded.

How will "effects" be measured?
- Higher satisfaction with the hospital experience?
- Less use of pain medication?
- Fewer calls to the nurses while in the hospital?
- An increased healing rate as measured by the length of stay in the hospital?
- A recognized spiritual significance to illness and recovery?
- Fewer lawsuits filed against the hospital?
- An increased motivation for medical follow-up?
- A more rapid payment of the bill?
- A change in life style which promotes health?
- A greater satisfaction with their physician?
- An increase in church attendance after dismissal?

As you become aware of all these variables and possibilities, I encourage you think about them as opportunities. Discouragement about complexity will only drain your energy and ignoring complexity will create problems at a later point.

How can you go about making a decision in regard to all these options? First, realize that no right answer exists. The question is, "How do you want to shape your research project?" You can make decisions about all these options as you judge necessary, but you must also be ready to explain those decisions in your report. Your consultants and colleagues can provide help as you seek to clarify your research question. You need to ask yourself as you make these decisions whether you are shaping the question in a way which will so sustain your interest that you can complete the project. Additionally, you will need to ask yourself about the practical details mentioned earlier: Can you get the data, and get them in a trustworthy form? Do you have the time and budget to do the study? Is there support in your setting for this work or will your superiors regard it as a distraction which takes you away from your primary duties? And are you ready for the worst possible outcome? Under what circumstances will social workers, parish pastors, patients, physicians, nurses, ministers, or fellow chaplains be grateful to or angry at you?

Let us suppose that during a period of time you sort through all these options and questions, moving toward increasing concreteness. You begin to know what you want to study based on your sense of emotional energy for the questions, availability of time and subjects, and existing relationships. For the sake of example, let us assume that your interest in "the effects of chaplains upon hospital patients" takes the shape of the following question: "Are male chaplains more effective than female chaplains in providing pastoral care to female patients in this hospital?" Notice that this question is more concrete: "chaplain" in the original statement has now become "male" and "female chaplains" and "hospital patients" has become "female hospital patients." Notice too that this concreteness requires your willingness to leave some options behind because parish pastors and male hospital patients will not be involved.

More options still must be left behind, however, as further definition, clarity, and power are achieved. Think, for example, about the implications of including all female hospital patients. Much diversity exists within this group, probably too much diversity for a good study. How can the group be narrowed? One solution would be to study a specific diagnostic group such as those with AIDS, cancer, or specific OB-GYN problems. A specification of one group depends, again, upon your interest, upon available subjects, and upon relationships which permit the design. For the sake of illustration, let us suppose that you further define your project as studying the following question: "Are male chaplains more effective than female chaplains in providing pastoral care to female cancer patients?" Now other options have been left behind because all non-cancer female patients will be excluded.

This question still possesses considerable breadth and variation. The issues of chaplaincy training and length of experience are unexplored. Additionally "female cancer patients" is still a diverse group. Will you be studying women with new diagnoses or terminal cancer patients? Will you further define your study group according to the organ system which is diseased? You will need to make some decision about this in order to reduce the variability within your study. And as you make that decision you need to keep in mind the need for an adequate number of subjects who fall within your chosen diagnostic group during an acceptable length of time.

So once again you narrow your study. Now, for sake of example, your research question becomes: "Are male chaplains with four or more units of CPE training more effective than female chaplains with comparable training in providing pastoral care to deteriorating gynecological cancer patients who have been admitted to the hospital for the second time in twelve months?" Now the ambiguity about chaplaincy training is clarified. A rather discrete patient group has also been identified, presumably with sufficient numbers to provide ample subjects.

Now another consideration comes into view because a difficult problem is hidden in this research question and will be apparent when it is converted into a research design. This last definition of the question moved the study into the realm of the near-terminal patient. How can data be gathered from the very ill, often terminal patients or from patients who die before final data are collected? Unless this question is answered satisfactorily, it will defeat the project. Perhaps the clearest answer to the problem is to impose still further specifications into the design which gather data for a very short, specific period of time.

Whatever the difficulties, benefits also exists in working with this patient group. One of the largest benefits is that the results can probably be generalized to other very ill patient groups. Research is valuable when results from a small group can be generalized to a larger population in a logical way. This generalizing process takes the place of studying every subject, a totally unmanageable task. This current project definition allows you to generalize your findings to other groups, such as all women with a GYN cancer or perhaps to all women who are dying from any chronic illness. Such generalization would need to be argued carefully but this definition of the question provides that opportunity and opens up a larger potential audience and number of journals that might be interested in your work.

The project definition is not yet complete, however. Now you must specify the quantitative aspect of the research question. The concern is, to put it simply, "What do you mean by `more effective' in your research question? How will `more effective' be measured?" Again, you can select weaker or stronger quantitative methods, and this choice should be based on the specifics of your situation. I will describe the various methods, from weaker to stronger, constructing for the sake of example a design which seems unmanageable to all except the most experienced researcher with a large budget.

You could gather an evaluation of pastoral care near the end of the data gathering period by inviting the patients to make a written statement which evaluates their pastoral care. You could then simply count those which express appreciation and those which do not and relate them to chaplain gender. The strength of this method is that it encourages free and spontaneous expression. It would be even more effective if the patients' reports were anonymous. But this approach also contains many weaknesses. Some patients do not express themselves well in writing and many may neglect your invitation. Some patients may not be able to write, due either to illiteracy or continued incapacity.

Three problems dominate this approach, however. The research question you have chosen involves program evaluation. In the evaluation process, this unstructured design can consciously or unconsciously encourage only the return of testimonials. Testimonials are not really research data because they are advertisements and propaganda. While helpful at some points, these materials will be quickly dismissed by editors and experienced researchers.

This problem is linked to a second. Can you reasonably assume that patients will freely provide an objective evaluation of pastoral care, particularly when no format or structure is provided? Does the average hospitalized patient possess that level of ego strength? Probably not! Instead, patients will provide socially acceptable answers, the answers they think are expected of them. A free-form, written statement would probably praise the work of everyone. After all, chaplains are men and women of God.

The third problem is even greater. What criteria are used by patients when they express their evaluation of pastoral care? Most researchers would argue that in this design, the criteria vary with each patient, making the task of analysis impossible. The research design creates no control on this variable. Patients could praise or disdain their pastoral care using many criteria, including, for example, a shared denominational affiliation, age, choice of words in a prayer, or even the hair style and appearance of the chaplain. Such responses use various criteria and some way must be found to create a uniform basis for evaluation.

If, despite all these difficulties you adopt this approach, the research question becomes: "Do deteriorating gynecological cancer patients undergoing their second admission in twelve months more frequently express written appreciation for pastoral care by trained male or trained female chaplains?" You then select a stronger quantitative methodology by constructing a standardized questionnaire for patient distribution. The standardization strengthens the quality of the data because all patients respond to the same questions, selecting an answer directly related to quantitative interpretation. If you elect this model, the research question becomes: "Using questionnaire xyz, do deteriorating gynecological cancer patients undergoing their second admission within twelve months provide more favorable scores for pastoral care by trained male chaplains or trained female chaplains?"

A third methodology, the strongest one, involves using published questionnaires. These questionnaires have been tested and evaluated and their performance has been sufficiently satisfactory to merit publication. In this way you build on the strength inherent in another's work. How can you find an applicable questionnaire? Reading the literature is important because authors tell you what they have used in similar situations and any problems they have uncovered. Additionally, you can look for applicable instruments in *The Mental Measurements Yearbook* or other descriptive sources. Again, consultation with knowledgeable consultants is essential.

As you work on questionnaire selection, think ahead to the time when all the data will be collected and analyzed. At that moment you will probably wish you had collected more information, used more than one questionnaire so that your research question could be examined from more than one perspective. This is an important insight. Gather as much data as possible, using multiple questionnaires. This effort must be balanced only with the estimated endurance and patience of the subjects. Again, if you identify multiple instruments, their potential contribution must be described in the research question.

Many additional variables and options must be investigated as the research question is developed for an actual project. You have probably thought of them while reading. I have been concerned with portraying the process rather than with completeness. The process slowly builds the foundation of the project. Clarity born out of exhaustive, careful thinking will bear fruit.

## CREATING THE HYPOTHESIS

Having created the research question, you must now hypothesize the answer. Yes, science is an answering process, but the data are collected and analyzed to confirm or deny your hypothesis. What, in your estimation, is the answer to the research question developed in this chapter? Will the data place more value on pastoral care from male or female chaplains? If you knew the answer, you would not need to conduct the study. You probably have a hunch, however, born out of past patient care experiences or shaped by your reading, thinking, or consultation. This hunch motivates the study.

Yet, the hypothesis is often one which states that no difference will exist between groups involved in the study. This is the classical "null hypothesis." In this instance, the null hypothesis would state that the gender of the chaplain created no statistically significant difference in the evaluation of pastoral care provided to deteriorating gynecological cancer patients who completed questionnaire xyz. When significant difference is uncovered (usually $p$ equal to or smaller than 0.05) then you can report that the "no difference" hypothesis was not confirmed and a difference does exist. We will discuss this further in chapter 6.

While you are finding your way through this process of creating the question, a process in which everything is connected to everything else, you should expect problems to emerge. Problems emerge both for every first-time researcher and for most who have accumulated extensive experience. These problems lead to confusion and discouragement. Finding your way through the maze of questions is difficult and what seems decided today is confused tomorrow. What seemed clear last week is unclear today. Expect it! This is simply the purifying of the research ideas as you move from conception to planning. You are working your way through the heart of the project. Later problems will emerge, of course, but they will not involve the confusion inherent in the planning process. And remember that this confusion and discouragement is worst in the first experience of research just as when you first learned to preach and to provide pastoral care or counseling. It will get easier with experience.

In summary, your research question needs to be shaped by fundamental principles and your management of situational variables. No single, right way exists. A time period of several months is often required to develop research questions. Give yourself that time for careful planning, knowing that you are writing the script and that future changes will be difficult.

# 5

# Seeking to Answer the
# Question: Research Design

**O**nce again the research task changes. Having tentatively identified the research question and stated the hypothesis, your task now is the construction of a design, a plan, which will test your hypothesis. As discussed in the last chapter, some design questions are already settled by the very wording of the research question. This chapter further refines research design concerns. At points my discussion will be limited because this book is a primer and you can read about detailed, technical matters in other sources.

The principal purpose of a research design is to produce objective data. The scientific approach moves beyond personal impression in order to see its subject matter "as it really is" and the purpose of the design is to accomplish this goal. The best scientific designs do not achieve complete objectivity, however. In 1927, Bertrand Russell sarcastically observed patterns of bias in research reports using animals as subjects:

> One may say broadly that all animals that have been carefully ob-
> served have behaved so as to confirm the philosophy in which the
> observer believed before his observations began. Nay, more, they
> have all displayed the national characteristics of the observer. Ani-
> mals studied by Americans rush about frantically, with an incredible
> display of hustle and pep, and at last achieve the desired results by
> chance. Animals observed by Germans sit still and think and at last
> achieve the solution out of their inner consciousness. To the plain
> man, such as the present writer, this situation is discouraging.

This amusing and exaggerated statement contains a grain of truth. Some elements of observer bias always enter into scientific activity. From time to time credible research reports emerge which others cannot duplicate, apparently because subjectivity biased the results.

Bias is a serious problem in theological work, including pastoral care and counseling research, because meager or ambiguous evidence invites scholars to project their own assumptions into the data. Albert Schweitzer commented on this problem in the broader field of theology and specifically in New Testament studies in *The Quest for the Historical Jesus*:

> Each successive epoch of theology found its own thoughts in Jesus.... But it was not only each epoch that found its reflection in Jesus, each individual created him in accordance with his own character. There is no historical task which so reveals a man's true self as the writing of a life of Jesus (1948, p. 4).

The task of a quantitative research design is to constrain such biases and to prevent them from completely destroying the reliability of scientific findings.

The capability of the design to produce trustworthy results is described as its *reliability*. A design and its data are reliable when the research process produces similar results when repeated in another setting and at another time. Reliability, therefore, rests on a stability in the research situation, a stability in which the data gathering is not victimized by shifting organizational and situational factors. Your research should be undertaken when "business as usual" prevails.

Research designs are built upon the clear identification of variables. A variable is any factor which impacts upon the research subjects with a likely influence upon the results. Such variables must be carefully identified so that their changes can be linked to variations in the results. In experimental research designs, you deliberately create a change in one selected variable (the independent variable) while continuing to track the others (dependent or response variables) to determine the effect of that change. In the research question developed in the previous chapter, you would gather data on many dependent/response variables while deliberately assigning male and female chaplains (the independent variable) to visit the gynecological cancer patients.

Research designs begin with the simple and move to the complex, a process which, as discussed in the preceding chapter, increases their power. A weak design produces data which can be interpreted as supportive of many different conclusions. Stronger, more complex designs eliminate multiple conclusions one by one until a conclusion concerning only your hypothesis remains. The data produced by these more complex designs may or may not confirm your hypothesis but they speak directly to it.

You may conclude from this that research uses only the strongest designs. This is not true. For example, a descriptive design, while lacking power, makes an important contribution when examining a new field of study. This design simply describes the variables and their interrelationship without any determination of cause and effect. Such an effort describes the geography of the interest area and sets the stage for more specialized causative studies.

Additionally, researchers often do not use the stronger designs because they pay an increasingly higher price as design strength increases. This price involves multiple, complex patient groups as well as increased time, personnel costs, and numbers of patients. These factors always influence what designs are possible. Your chosen research design, therefore, will be a compromise, using the strongest possible design within circumstantial constraints such as budget, time, and the availability of subjects.

We can use the research question from the preceding chapter to illustrate the movement from a simple to a complex design with increasing strength. Do female chaplains deliver better pastoral care to the designated patient group? A descriptive study is weak, simply describing how many chaplains and patients exist, their gender, and other related demographic data. The study also describes the number of pastoral care visits made and the related gender data. Such a study cannot, however, answer the question. A design which demonstrates cause and effect is needed.

What design features are necessary to draw conclusions about causation? The first is a two-situational or two-group study. To demonstrate cause and effect, you need to manipulate the chosen independent variable to test for its effect. You need data from a situation in which this manipulation occurs as well as from one in which it does not occur. This provides a comparison and allows a conclusion about cause and effect. This can be accomplished in some situations by a single-group study in which baseline data are gathered and then the selected independent variable is manipulated. You can argue that subsequent changes in the data were caused by your action. This is particularly true if you withdraw the change, allow the data to return to baseline and then introduce the change a second time with the same results. This is described in research literature as the ABAB design (A = baseline and B = experiment by manipulating the variable).

The other way to demonstrate cause and effect requires at least two groups. You manipulate the chosen variable in the one group but not in the other. Since both groups are identical in all other ways, you argue that data differences between the groups are due to your action. Either of these two designs demonstrates cause and effect and often both are used to provide a double comparison.

The second design feature necessary to demonstrate a causal connection involves randomness. Randomness insures that the patient assignment to the groups is not affected by bias, such as assigning all the difficult cases to one group. In our example, random selection is used either to assign patients to the participating chaplains or to assign the chaplains to the patients. Only this random process will convince editors and the skeptical reader that sufficient objectivity exists to allow for a conclusion about causal connections.

Random assignment is accomplished in many ways. You can use a random numbers table from the appendices of a research or statistics book. Beginning with 1, simply assign each participating chaplain a number. Then select a column in the table and, with a list of patients in hand, move downward. When you come to a number which designates a chaplain, he or she is assigned the next patient. Think clearly about how this will work because you should not deviate from this assignment process once you have begun. Plan what you will do if, for example, a participating chaplain is ill for several days or takes a vacation. Other methods which assure randomness include the use of dice or the coin toss (assuming only two participants). Figure 1 diagrams this two-group design. Assuming that the data support the hypothesis, you can argue for cause and effect.

You will experience some difficulty in arguing a causal connection, however, because the design is relatively weak. When you describe your results, the skeptics will understand your design, but will wonder whether any objective evidence exists that documents the benefits to the patients. You see, it is possible that female patients simply praise female chaplains more highly without any pastoral care benefits ever existing. How do you know the patients are describing true improvement? The above design cannot determine whether the patients are in fact improved or are only saying so. What is necessary to create an answer?

## FIGURE 1

### A Two-Group Study With Post-Experiment Data
### (Random Assignment to Groups)

Group 1
(Female Chaplain)                    X X X X X X X X X X o$^1$

Group 2
(Male Chaplain)                      X X X X X X X X X X o$^1$

X represents pastoral care visits; o represents data gathering. The number of X's (10) are for example only. o$^1$ represents self-report data from patients concerning evaluation of pastoral care.

The design requires an independent, free-standing evaluation of the patient at admission, an evaluation which is repeated at the end of the study. This evaluation provides objective evidence of changes in the patient's status. How can such an evaluation be accomplished? Perhaps the patient can complete evaluation questionnaires or a trained interviewer can talk with the patient in structured interviews. In either case, you must determine the content of this pretest-posttest, construct the instrument or interview, and arrange to manage the process in an objective way. Here, as in all social sciences, this increased power exacts a high price in complexity, time, and money. Figure 2 illustrates this design.

## FIGURE 2

### Figure 1 Experiment With Added Pre-Post Experiment Evaluator Data (Random Assignment to Groups)

Group 1
(Female Chaplain) $o^2$ X X X X X X X X X X X $o^1$ $o^2$

Group 2
(Male Chaplain) $o^2$ X X X X X X X X X X X $o^1$ $o^2$

$o^2$ represents pre-post experiment evaluator data.

But now another possibility emerges. As noted above, many studies use not only a pretest-posttest measure or interview but also an untreated group as a second comparison. This additional group, which receives no pastoral care but completes the pretest-posttest, further strengthens the design. Data from this group will allow you to determine the benefits of pastoral care because you are measuring a group which receives none. Data from this group form another baseline, a no-treatment baseline against which the male and female chaplain data can be understood. This strengthens the design because, if the data would support it, you could argue that pastoral care to gynecological patients from male chaplains is better than nothing according to data from the untreated group, but that female chaplains are more effective. If you use this three-group design, you must have access to a sufficient patient population of gynecological cancer patients and assignments to each group must still be made randomly. This design is shown in Figure 3.

## FIGURE 3

### Figure 2 Experiment With Added No-Treatment Group (Random Assignment to Groups)

No-Treatment Group $o^2$ $o^2$

Group 1
(Female Chaplain) $o^2$ X X X X X X X X X X X $o^1$ $o^2$

Group 2
(Male Chaplain) $o^2$ X X X X X X X X X X X $o^1$ $o^2$

At this juncture you may realize that you ought to research the benefits of pastoral care by chaplains generally prior to undertaking this gender-oriented project. After all, you say, let's study first questions first. Let's determine if pastoral care makes any difference no matter what the gender of the provider, and then let's study whether one gender is better for some patients than the other. You are accurate in that observation. As so often happens, the most complex research problems attract attention first. Working on these complex problems leads you to realize that prior questions and problems exist. In fact, this gender-related project is premature until you have documented that pastoral care makes a contribution, no matter what the gender of the provider. If you actually planned to carry out this project now, you would set aside this current effort and start with a demonstration of the effects of any pastoral care. When that project was successfully completed, you would return to the gender-related project.

But suppose that while reading the literature, you discover an article reporting the beneficial effects of pastoral care. The design is strong and the results solid. Your present study could build on that effort, and then you could proceed without going back to the basic issue.

The design illustrated in Figure 3 can be strengthened even further. Notice that one group only reaches the pretest- posttest while the other two groups receive regularly scheduled pastoral care. Some skeptics will argue that your positive results are caused by the increased attention to the two treatment groups. They will argue that the results do not measure the impact of pastoral care but of chaplains who regularly visit patients and talk nicely to them. Researchers describe these benefits due to increased attention as the Hawthorne Effect.

A stronger design results if you control for the impact of increased attention. You accomplish this control by introducing a behavioral placebo into the no-treatment group which avoids the type of pastoral care tested with the other groups. Planning this placebo requires you to define exactly the nature and structure of the pastoral care. With that definition in hand, you create a design in which the no-treatment group receives attention but not the pastoral care. They receive the same number of visits for the same number of minutes, but only attention must be provided. How can this be accomplished?

Again, no right formula exists, but here are two possible solutions. A specially trained chaplaincy volunteer can visit this group with the same frequency received by the other groups but only "pass the time of day" inquiring about mundane matters and practical details. Another possibility involves chaplains themselves whose visits could include a structured program of Bible reading, recorded meditations, or the playing of hymns with minimum personal conversation. This would provide attention but not the aspects of pastoral care tested in the other groups. If you adopt this strengthened design, the structure looks like Figure 4.

## FIGURE 4
### Figure 3 Experience With Added Placebo Pastoral Care
### (Random Assignment to Groups)

No-Treatment Group $\qquad$ $o^2$ Y Y Y Y Y Y Y Y Y Y $o^1$ $o^2$

Group 1
(Female Chaplain) $\qquad$ $o^2$ X X X X X X X X X X $o^1$ $o^2$

Group 2
(Male Chaplain) $\qquad$ $o^2$ X X X X X X X X X X $o^1$ $o^2$

Y represents placebo pastoral care.

Now look at the design diagram in Figure 4 and begin to imagine how this will work. What problems exist in the design or in practical details? The design can be strengthened by yet one more modification. Will male or female persons provide the placebo pastoral care to the no-treatment group? Gender is fundamental to the entire study and confusion should not exist concerning this in the no-treatment group. The design confusion is easily clarified by adding an additional no-treatment group so that one exists for a female chaplain or volunteer and one for a male chaplain or volunteer. Now you have gender-matched comparison groups, a design depicted in Figure 5.

## FIGURE 5
### Figure 4 Experiment With Additional No-Treatment Groups
### (Random Assignment to Groups)

No-Treatment Group
(Female Volunteer
or Chaplain) $\qquad$ $o^2$ Y Y Y Y Y Y Y Y Y Y $o^1$ $o^2$

No-Treatment Group
(Male Volunteer or
Chaplain) $\qquad$ $o^2$ Y Y Y Y Y Y Y Y Y Y $o^1$ $o^2$

Group 1
(Female Chaplain) $\qquad$ $o^2$ X X X X X X X X X X $o^1$ $o^2$

Group 2
(Female Chaplain) $\qquad$ $o^2$ X X X X X X X X X X $o^1$ $o^2$

In this section, I have sought to demonstrate how research designs develop as a result of scientific skepticism. As the designs reflect more and more complexity, they become overwhelming, flooding your abilities, time, budget, available personnel resources, or cadre of patients. At the point of saturation, you must make a decision about how much complexity the project staff, including yourself, can tolerate. An extraordinarily strong research design is useless if it can not be completed. Choose a design you can manage and simply explain the limits you faced in the written report.

The data-gathering instrument is part of the research design. Many excellent books are available and I will not describe the process except to note one area of concern. The process of creating a questionnaire involves a decision about how the data will be scaled or classified. Four data classifications exist and they determine what statistical tests can be used in the process of analysis. I will describe these scales from the least sophisticated to the most accurate and useful. Statistical textbooks and consultants can help you with the details of this matter.

A *nominal* scale, the simplest, collects responses in arbitrary categories. The responses sort or label objects, people, or opinions. For example, people are either church members or nonmembers. No relative standing within the groups is possible in the nominal scale. Your questionnaire about pastoral care would create a nominal scale response if you asked, "Was pastoral care from the chaplain helpful? Yes or no?"

The *ordinal* scale not only categorizes but also ranks responses on the basis of their relative standing within the group. Suppose that an item in your research read, "Taken as a whole, how helpful was pastoral care from the Chaplain? Very helpful, fairly helpful, somewhat helpful, not helpful." Now you know more than in the nominal scale. You know the relative positions of the respondents. Those who respond that pastoral care was "very helpful" can be scored higher than those who said it was "helpful."

The *interval* scale provides more data still. In addition to categorizing data (nominal) into relative position (ordinal), this scale contains equal distance or difference between its units. Thermometer measurement of temperature is a typical example. The difference between 40° and 50° is the same as the difference between 10° and 20° since the units of measurements are consistent.

The *ratio* scale is the most powerful because, in addition to nominal, ordinal, and interval characteristics, the measurements are taken from a true zero point. Weight measurement provides an example. Not only is the difference between 10 and 20 pounds the same as 40 and 50 pounds, but you know that 40 pounds is twice as heavy as 20 pounds. This observation uses a ratio scale because zero pounds consist of no weight at all. This is not true of the temperature example. Zero degrees is an arbitrary point because, as a matter of fact, it is different for Fahrenheit and Centigrade scales.

Social sciences seldom are able to use interval or ratio scales because their data do not lend themselves to either scale. Constructing ordinal scales is very important, however, because these data will facilitate your analytical process.

One final observation is important. When you complete your design, perform a pilot project. Give the design a test run with a limited number of subjects, performing data collection and analysis. In this way, you can be assured that the research process will actually work and produce trustworthy data.

In summary, I have repeatedly emphasized two themes in this section. It is time to repeat them. First, do not be surprised if you are overwhelmed by the complexity of building a research design. This task is another point at which you can "sink down in the mud" of confusion and discouragement. I have not described these more elaborate, powerful designs with the assumption that you will immediately understand and use them. Rather, their description here helps you experience the reasoning process which shapes the building of research designs. At the same time, I hope you have grasped something of the interrelatedness of the entire research process.

Second, the use of a research consultant in building a design is mandatory for the inexperienced. Let your consultant help you with advice. Raise your questions. The scientific process involves a point of view which must be caught through experience and struggle. Keep working to capture that scientific methodology by reading but also by talking with a knowledgeable consultant.

# 6

# Working With the Data

Y ou have worked long and hard to produce good quantitative data. This effort has focused upon creating numbers which can be concretely analyzed, compared, and interpreted. These data have placed you in a strong position when compared with narrative or testimonial responses. Now the time has come to reap the benefits. The data are collected! Now what must you do?

The clear answer is that you must analyze the data. That can be a larger and more complicated task than first imagined, however. Data come in many different forms and through many different research designs. These character-istics, plus the number of respondents, influence the choice of statistical tests. Consequently, you must continue to talk to your consultant. What test is appropriate for these data? Hopefully this is not your first conversation about data analysis. Wisdom dictates that planning for data analysis takes place during the design phase of the project. If planning has taken place at that time, then your analysis problems are already under control.

In this chapter, I do not plan to describe the various statistical and analyti-cal processes. Many good books are available (e.g., Dowdy & Wearden, 1991). Rather, I will describe some selected fundamental mathematical concepts. This will help you get inside the mathematical mind and create an initial common ground between your consultant and yourself. I will discuss measures of central tendency, measures of central dispersion, and the concept of statistically significant difference.

## MEASURES OF CENTRAL TENDENCY

This name is applied to the mean, median, and mode of data. Fundamen-tally, they all in their own way describe the center location of the data, the point around which the data cluster. They describe the inward tendency of the results.

The mean is calculated by dividing the sum of the scores by the total number of scores. The median is a point on a measurement scale above which lie exactly half of the scores and below which lie the other half. The mode, a third measure of central tendency, is the value or score which occurs with the most frequency in the data.

Each of these measures is a helpful description of the data, particularly when large variations occur. In your research project concerning gender of the chaplain, suppose you gather financial income data from the patients. The data report that 99 subjects report an income of $30,000, but one subject is a millionaire. The mean income for the group is $39,700 but this is misleading because only one subject is above $30,000. The median and mode are more helpful here; both are $30,000, but they conceal the fact that one subject was a millionaire. Thus these multiple mathematical expressions each possess benefits and disadvantages. Despite the versatility of these three measures of central tendency, the mean is the most frequently reported and the basis for additional mathematical calculations.

## MEASURES OF CENTRAL DISPERSION

The measures of central tendency describe the various center points of the data, points around which the data cluster. These descriptors by themselves are incomplete and can be misleading because they do not describe the amount of spread in the data. For example, the mean of 50 represents 43 and 55 as well as 25 and 75. This matter is important because while the central tendency measurements describe the center point, some descriptor is needed to depict how representative this mean is of the total data. Clearly a mean of 50 is more closely representative of data values of 45 and 55 than of 25 and 75. The descriptors which describe the data spread are measures of central dispersion.

The range is a natural measure of dispersion. The range is composed of the largest and smallest value in the data set. This simple measure has many disadvantages, the most serious being that it relies completely on two values, the highest and the lowest.

How could all scores in the data set be involved in measuring the dispersion? Such a mechanism would be the counterpart to the mean in the measures of central tendency. The most common approach begins by measuring the deviation of each score from the mean, whether it is positive or negative (above or below the mean). This new list of numbers which describes deviation from the mean can be summed and divided by the total number of scores. This sounds familiar because it follows the same procedure as finding the mean. The result of adding this list of deviations from the mean and dividing by the total number of scores produces a *mean deviation.*

Mean deviation in itself is not useful, however, because the design (the positive or negative quality) of the number has been ignored. Statisticians find this troublesome and they prefer to change all numbers into positive ones as they work with them. They accomplish this by squaring them. All squared numbers (the number multiplied by itself) are positive. This additional step, therefore, calculates the deviation from the mean and squares that number. These squared numbers are then summed and divided by the total number of scores. This process produces a measure of dispersion called the *variance.* From time to time this measure is reported in research articles. Usually the variance is itself a stepping stone to the most common statistic of dispersion because it has created another problem. When the number is squared, the unit descriptions are also squared (i.e., inches become square inches). This is easily corrected by taking the square root of the variance. Now the original unit of measure is restored and you have calculated the most common measure of dispersion, the *standard deviation.* It is frequently reported in data tables with the mean, one representing the measure of central tendency and the other the measure of central dispersion. These two measures become the basis for most of the statistical tests which search for the presence of statistically significant differences.

## STATISTICALLY SIGNIFICANT DIFFERENCE

The preceding measurement processes describe characteristics of data in concrete form. Scientists, however, are not satisfied with mere description. They wish to make statements about the effects of experimental actions upon the subjects, particularly that part of the subject's life under study. This is understandable because the statistical descriptions in your results may not represent the next set of subjects because they may be due to chance. The scientist wants to make a statement such as, "The difference between the two groups previous to and following the experimental intervention is of such magnitude that we cannot reasonably ascribe it to chance variation." That statement tells us something about this part of reality and the reader can assume that a second study could logically produce approximately the same results. This is a decided advance over mere description.

Research possesses a mathematical process for determining whether the difference is large enough that it is not likely to be due to a random, chance event. This process determines the "*p* value" (for probability) and establishes the chance (in the form of percentage) that the difference is just random and thus not to be expected again. Usually the acceptable level is 0.05 (five chances in 100); then you are in an even stronger position to claim that the difference is due to your experimental intervention. Remember our discussion in an earlier chapter in which we stated that science never proves anything. Here you see the background to that statement. The very structure of the scientific mathematical process describes proof only in terms of probability.

How can this concept be explained further? The first step is to realize that the scientific method always looks for difference but expects to find none. In science the burden of proof is always on the one who states that a difference exists. Consequently, the improved pastoral care to gynecological patients from female chaplains as discussed previously really requires the assumption that no difference will exist between pastoral care given by males and females. This is the traditional "null hypothesis." If a difference is found, particularly at or below the 5% probability limit, then the $p$ value registers your surprise. Thus, the smaller the $p$ value (0.04, 0.03, 0.02, 0.01, 0.009, etc.), the less tenable the null hypothesis and the more likely that the findings are not due to chance. The $p$ value is usually discussed as a confidence level, confidence, that is, that the findings are not due to chance. Therefore, although we seek to establish a gender-linked difference in pastoral care, we work from an assumption that no difference exists until demonstrated otherwise by a $p$ value of 0.05 or smaller.

All of this can be displayed in graphic form. Let us suppose that the gender issue is completely irrelevant and immaterial to quality pastoral care to gynecological cancer patients. If that is so, the responses to your questionnaire from all patient groups would be random and produce a normal distribution curve (Figure 1). In that instance, most of the responses would fall in the middle of the range set up in your questionnaire. Few would choose the extreme upper or lower ranges of "very helpful" or "not helpful." In fact, as you see from the normal curve in Figure 1, a predictable percentage of responses would fall in those various ranges if a normal distribution or "bell-shaped curve" were created. Now in order to produce results at or below the 0.05 $p$-value, a sufficient number of responses from the group with a female chaplain will have to shift to the right or to the left, producing not a bell-shaped curve but a skewed curve as in Figure 2. The exact number of patient responses or the amount of shift required depends on the number of points on the scale and the number of respondents. This is beyond the scope of this book, but the graphic presentation can help you visualize the process. Consult research books for further discussion.

I have discussed measures of central tendency and dispersion and the concept of statistically significant difference. A grasp of these concepts will provide some common understanding between your consultant and yourself. Items that remain for discussion with your consultant include choice of the appropriate statistical tests and the data arrangement required for analysis. When the test results are back, your consultant can also help you with appropriate interpretation. Ask your questions and let the consultant help you.

In summary, the crowning jewel in quantitative research is data analysis and the appropriate interpretation of the results. All previous work had pointed toward this culmination. Conversely, analysis of results will be no better than the care taken during the rest of the project. With results in hand, you are ready for the final step—writing the journal article. I will address that in the next chapter.

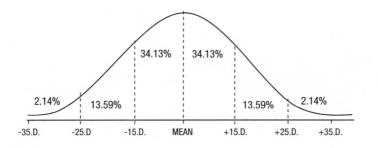

FIGURE 1

*A normal distribution as represented by a Bell-Shaped Curve.*

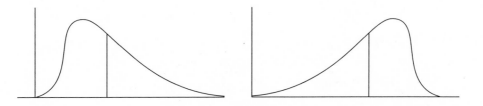

FIGURE 2

*Two skewed curves indicating more extreme responses
than in the normal distribution.*

# 7 | Writing the Results

**Y**ou finished the project! You gained significant insights into your questions. Now other duties demand your attention and you seek relief from the research struggle.

In reality, relief is not at hand! Instead, you face the greatest temptation in your research process, the temptation not to report the project in writing. If you are working in a degree program, you know about the writing task ahead because your advisor and review committee require a written document. The scientific community possesses the same standards. In a strict sense, research becomes research only when published.

The challenge of writing the journal article calls for unique skills. All the skills needed to narrow the interest area into a research question, to design a project to answer the question, to gather and interpret the data, are not what you need now. Now you need technical writing skills. The challenge presented by the need for these skills constitutes the essence of the difficulty and of the temptation to proceed no further. If the writing challenge seems overwhelming, remember that the first experience is always the worst. Even so, experienced researchers believe that writing consumes one-fourth to one-third of the entire energy devoted to a project. Producing good writing is hard work.

This chapter provides resources to cope with this struggle. I will give particular attention to choosing appropriate journals, writing the sections of the research article, and coping with concerns of style and grammar.

## JOURNAL IDENTIFICATION

The selection of potential journals must be made before writing begins for two reasons. The first is simple: journals possess different editorial styles and you need to be aware of these differences as you put the manuscript together. Obtain an "Instructions to Authors" statement from each journal in which you are interested and follow the guidelines carefully. Editors typically publish these at least once each year in the journal.

The second and more complicated reason for audience identification involves strategy. A painful personal experience will illustrate the importance of this strategy. In my first research project, I studied task importance and time usage among clergy in my denomination. During the study I fantasized that my results would be published in the only denominational periodical. Having completed the project, I sent off the finished product and settled back to await my reward. They rejected my manuscript. They did not publish tables (my submission naively contained many) and my study was not interesting to them. I was crushed and hurt. What could I do now? I had only two alternatives: give up or undertake an enormous rewriting process. The experience taught me a lesson: before writing, identify a broad spectrum of journals to which you can submit your work. This strategy has been successful for me with a recent study which now has been accepted for publication after five rejections. Look through various issues of the journals and identify those which you believe could be interested in your work, making a list. Indexed and abstracted journals usually set higher standards for manuscript acceptance, making them more sophisticated. You should place these journals near the top of your list if you have a strong project.

And now a word about manuscript rejections! Researchers believe that 70% of the manuscripts are eventually published if the author persists. An initial rejection or two is common. Do not take the rejection personally even though that temptation is ever- present. Editors do not insult contributors although the popular press sometimes characterizes them in this way. Take the reviewer's feedback seriously. If no comments are provided, you can request them from the editor. Journals have many reasons for refusing articles. They may have recently accepted or published a similar article. The article, despite your best efforts, may lie outside their interests. Your contribution may have been reviewed by persons who were disinterested in or biased against your subject matter.

Apart from these issues, manuscripts are rejected because the research design was not carefully planned or executed. Perhaps important variables were not adequately identified or the data were collected in problematic form. Research design mistakes cannot be corrected after the data are collected and you need to find a journal less sensitive to these issues.

If you receive a rejection, be prepared to make any necessary changes and send the article out again within thirty days. Keep the momentum up; keep the manuscript in front of editors.

An ethical issue is also present here. Never send the same manuscript to more than one journal at a time. Editors require that the material not be under consideration elsewhere while they review it.

## WRITING THE SECTIONS OF THE ARTICLE

Most research journal articles are composed of four parts: introduction, methodology, results, and discussion. Some journals allow for a conclusion section, and many require an abstract which is placed at the beginning as a summary. Most researchers write these sections separately, welding them together in the latter part of the process.

You can write the literature review first. This review placed at the end of the introduction and written in past tense, reports relevant findings from other studies. Report your evaluation of and perspectives on these studies along with the research questions which you have explored. Generally, this material requires only a few paragraphs and can be drafted even before data analysis is complete.

The methodology section is often written next. Using verbs in past tense, describe your research design. Make this section strictly a report of relevant activities: you sent questionnaires, interviewed persons, or conducted tests. Carefully describe any unique questionnaires, paper-and-pencil instruments, or equipment you used.

The results section is usually created next. Using present tense verbs, report the number of questionnaires returned, interviews conducted, and the demographics of the respondents. Focus upon the data created by the project. Do not wander into discussion of the results; record thoughts for discussion in note form for that later section. Simply report the findings. Try to limit the number of tables to three or fewer. Journals calculate their costs per page, and tables are expensive because they take up room. Look at sample articles in quality journals and note how specific data are managed by experienced authors.

Most researchers agree that the introduction and the discussion sections are the most important and difficult to write. Many write these sections at this point, relying upon notes they have made for themselves. Both sections are written in the present tense. I will discuss the introduction first.

The introduction must attract the reader's attention. This is usually achieved by statements which convince the reader that your research addresses an important issue or problem. Busy readers scan their journals quickly, spending time only with those articles which catch their attention.

The first introductory sentence is crucial. Make it short and pithy. Choose an active verb and avoid clauses. The best lead sentence is often one which requires no commas. This sentence, which then functions as the topic sentence of the paragraph, is amplified, expanded, and explained in those which follow. After one or two paragraphs, this introduction leads into the literature review.

Read through some introductions in the journals. Some will constitute good writing, but others will be poorly done because some scientists are poor writers. You can practice your writing skills by improving their introductions.

The discussion section presents its own difficulties. Here you discuss your results, linking them to previous studies, noting their implications, and suggesting new research questions for the professional community. This calls for professional discernment and skill in order to illumine the meaning of your findings.

The discussion section often begins with a paragraph which clearly states how the data in the results section answer the research questions. This ties the research report together. The findings entitle you to make some claims, but you must also be alert to unrealistic assertions about them. As a general rule, be conservative in your claims.

After this paragraph, you should comment on important or unusual data characteristics, beginning with that which was presented first in the results section. The discussion section can end by noting limitations implicit in the findings and by raising additional questions for research.

The abstract is written last. Limited to 100-150 words, it can use phrases or sentences from the article, reflecting its four parts. Tell the reader the results in summary form. Avoid statements such as "implications are discussed." Remember that many will only read the abstract, lacking the time for detailed examination of your work.

## COPING WITH CONCERNS OF STYLE AND GRAMMAR

Why should you struggle with problems of style and grammar? Simply because good writing will help you publish and because no one writes well without giving attention to these matters. The journal editor and reviewers of your manuscript will be prejudiced against your contribution if reading it is hard work and confusing. They know that poor writing will also tax the subscribers and cause them to stop reading the journal.

Throughout the writing process you confront constant problems of paragraph and sentence construction. All of these problems essentially resolve into the need to communicate the content in clear language without wordiness. This requires a number of skills. First, you must learn to be objective about your own writing. No doubt your first draft looks good to you. You read it over and can make only a few improvements. And yet, it is a first draft. You wonder if it really is that good. How can you lift your own "blindness" to your work?

Here are two behaviors with which you can begin. First, go back to a written draft you created some months ago. The content really does not matter. Read over the draft and begin making changes to improve the style and cut out the wordiness. Notice how you can feel more objective about this writing simply because time has passed. With increased practice, this objectivity can be achieved after you set aside freshly written material for an hour.

The second helpful behavior is simply to dictate a few pages of material for typing. With the transcript in hand, you will soon see the wordiness. Verbal dictation is usually outrageously wordy and the typescript creates an opportunity to identify and reduce this excess.

After you begin this process, I recommend another. Read a few books about technical writing. They will further sensitize you to good and poor writing. Then begin to read journal articles, not necessarily for content, but to examine them for good and poor writing, for clear and confusing grammar. Your future as a good writer rests with the development of that critical eye. And then after you have begun to read critically the writings of others and to struggle with your own, refresh your memory about grammatical construction. In the end, knowledge about parts of speech and old-fashioned English grammar make writing easier.

Having described a process by which you can become a better writer, I will make two contributions to this process in the remainder of this chapter. Focusing first upon paragraph construction, I will share the five drafts of this chapter's opening paragraphs. This will help you grasp the process of writing, particularly as it applies to an introduction. Later, I will discuss some problems of sentence construction.

I revised this chapter's two opening paragraphs three times. This redrafting process was my effort to attain my own goals for an introduction. These revisions are reproduced below along with process comments. Here is the first draft of the chapter's opening paragraphs.

## FIRST DRAFT

> Upon arrival at this point in the research process, you are tempted to be relieved. This has been a difficult process, particularly if it was your first research effort. Perhaps you have gained significant insights into the research question. You are tempted to feel that you are nearly finished.
>
> If your research is part of a degree program, you know that the process is not finished. Now the research project must be written. Even if your work is not part of a degree program, it still needs to be written and reported to the professional community.

I have put something down and that is better than a blank page. Like most first draft writing, however, it is not in finished form and will probably never be published. As I reviewed this first draft material later, I realized that the first sentence did not seize the reader's attention and that the entire tone appeared tentative, in part because the first two sentences used passive verb forms. The two paragraphs were completely rewritten the next day.

## SECOND DRAFT

> Relief is at hand! You have finished the project! Perhaps you have gained significant insights into your research question. Now, other duties demand your attention and you are ready to move on.
>
> In reality, you now stand at the point of greatest temptation, the temptation to take the project no further and to neglect reporting it in the professional literature. Many novice researchers give into that temptation and never complete the project. If your work has been part of a degree program, you know that the project must be described in writing. It is required. That requirement is the standard in the scientific community. Research is not research until it is published.

I have written two new paragraphs although the ideas remain. The sentences in the first paragraph are shorter and capture the reader's attention by commenting on the needed sense of relief. I eliminated the passive verb forms. The second paragraph links this search for relief to the temptation to give up on the publication effort. As in the earlier draft, the paragraph uses the need to create a written document in degree programs as the standard for all research. These paragraphs appear better suited as a chapter beginning and some attention to stylistic and grammatical concerns are appropriate. A few days later some stylistic changes were made.

## THIRD DRAFT

> You finished the project! You gained significant insights into your questions. Now other duties demand your attention and you seek relief from the research struggle.
>
> In reality, relief is not at hand! Instead, you face the greatest temptation in your research process, the temptation not to report the project in writing. You know about the writing task ahead if your work is part of a degree program because your advisor and review committee require a written document. The scientific community possesses the same standards. Research becomes research only when published.

This product appeared at the head of this chapter. Adjustments in this draft included sentence and vocabulary changes. First the statement "Relief is at hand" was moved to the end of the paragraph to create a compound sentence. I felt it was wiser to speak first to the "finished" character of the project and then pick up the sense of relief. Second, the perfect verb forms, "have finished" and "have gained," were reduced to past tense: "finished" and "gained." This shortened and simplified the sentences, increasing their impact.

In the second paragraph, the theme of "relief" was immediately reintroduced and various word changes made. The sentence about novice researchers was dropped because it served no purpose. "That requirement is" was modified to read, "The scientific community possesses." This latter sentence abandons the "to be" verb and substitutes a more robust sentence.

These materials represent the hard work of writing the introductory paragraphs. Equally hard work is needed to produce meaningful materials from the entire first draft.

I will conclude this chapter by addressing the challenge of sentence construction and use an example. The example is a mass of entangled dictated words in the first draft of a semi-annual report to a college president. The president, already aware of the department's ethics grant, is given an update in this report. Here is the dictated sentence.

> The ethics grant is in its second year, and while the faculty ethicist provided cannot be guaranteed for continuation, and therefore is unable to attract a full-time person, several of our part- time faculty have combined to provide 20% or more equivalency to give the Department significant increase in teaching effort.

This 50 word sentence, if it can be called that, has multiple problems. Like much dictation, the speaker gets bogged down in clauses and forgets the beginning of the sentence. Most of the sentence is confused and impossible to understand grammatically. No editor would publish it. How can this sentence be reworked into a rigorous, clear, concise statement?

As I have struggled with my first drafts, I have learned not to make small changes. Take the first draft in hand and be ready to completely rewrite the narrative. I often rewrite material in longhand to achieve spontaneous insights concerning sentence structure. This also encourages larger vocabulary usage, resulting in clearer and more rigorous prose. In this first rewriting endeavor, a more clear and meaningful sentence demonstrates success. Here is what the author was trying to say:

> The ethics grant, now in its second year, has stimulated a 20% increase in teaching effort from parish-based faculty despite the difficulty in filling the grant's full-time faculty position because continuation funding cannot be guaranteed at the end of the grant.

Many difficulties still exist with this sentence, but the meaning is clearer. The sentence reports that a grant was received last year which created a new faculty position, a position which is difficult to fill because it is temporary. However, the grant has had other beneficial efforts because it has funded several parish-based faculty who have increased their teaching time. Their joint efforts have increased the department's teaching by 20%. The original sentence used 50 words and unclear grammar; the new sentence is better writing.

What further refinements are possible? Further work seems necessary because the concluding phrase of the sentence, "because continuation funding cannot be guaranteed at the end of the grant," seems a dangling group of words. Perhaps the sentence would be more rigorous if the clause concerning the full-time position were placed first. This is the result:

> The ethics grant, now in its second year, experiences difficulty in filling the temporary full-time faculty position although various parish faculty have increased their efforts so that the Department's teaching has risen 20%.

This construction of 33 words seems successful because the sentence is shorter and clearer. A new problem is created, however, because the negative problem with the full-time faculty position is placed first in the sentence. This order needs reversal again because positive benefits should be stated first.

The sentence also conveys two thoughts concerning the grant. Perhaps both clarity and conciseness would be enhanced with two sentences. This effort produces the following results:

> The ethics grant, now in its second year, produced a 20% increase in teaching through the combined efforts of several parish faculty.

> We have not filled the full-time faculty position because continuation after the grant cannot be guaranteed.

These sentences are now more readable and manageable. Their shortness allows for more elaboration and flexibility. The positive results of the grant are described first, the unfilled position reported at the end.

These sentences contain 38 words, however. Can other refinements increase the rigor by reducing the wordiness? Two areas invite attention. The first is the parenthetical phrase, "now in its second year," and the double use of the word "not" in the second sentence. Reworking the sentences with this in mind produces these results:

> The second year of the ethics grant supported several parish faculty whose combined efforts produced a 20% increase in teaching. The full-time faculty position remained open because continuation funding is uncertain.

This effort creates a 31-word result. Can this be further reduced for increased economy and clarity?

One phrase still seems loose and wordy, namely "efforts produced a 20% increase in teaching." The prepositional phrase is unnecessary if reconstructed into "efforts increase teaching 20%." We now have two sentences with rigor composed of 28 words:

> The second year of the ethics grant supported several parish faculty whose combined efforts increased teaching 20%. The full-time faculty position remained open because continuation funding is uncertain.

These two sentences are more clear, concise, and rigorous than the original monstrosity with which we began. Additional changes could be necessary depending upon the syntax of the paragraph in which it appears, but this process helps you understand the hard work which produces good writing.

This rewriting process is exhausting and is another point at which you can become confused and discouraged. All this writing and rewriting, it may seem to you, takes too much time. You may find that your skills are weak and that you possess little experience. In such a situation, remember that approximately one-fourth of the total energy for a project is focused upon the writing process. Also remember that the first time is the worst. Continue to cultivate these skills and writing will become easier.

And now one final word. Send a final draft of the manuscript to a number of your colleagues for review and feedback. Choose those whom you believe can be constructively critical. Never send an article to an editor without this peer review. The journal reviewers will likely give you the feedback you should have gotten from your colleagues, rejecting the article in the process.

In summary, writing well is hard work. Everyone who publishes learns these skills by experience or training. A writing consultant can be helpful and save you time and energy. Invite the consultant to review your manuscript when you circulate it to colleagues.

You should be able to obtain feedback from these informal reviews in a couple of weeks. Take it seriously, although you need not adopt all advice given to you. Make these decisions, put the manuscript in final form, and send it to your journal of choice.

But your work may not be finished yet. Many journals accept articles on condition that the authors make some revisions. Make the revisions and return the article as instructed. Usually relief is then at hand. You have finished the project. In due time you will see your name in print. The only remaining task is to circulate reprints to colleagues and others who are interested

# PART 2

# Qualitative Approaches

*by*
*Hilary E. Bender*
*and*
*Merle R. Jordan*

# 8

# Context for Qualitative Research

Pastoral caregivers spend much of their time listening empathically to parishioners, clients, hospital patients, and others to whom they minister. They seek to get inside the world of experience of others, to hear their voices, and to empower those voices for their fullest expression. Qualitative research invites parish clergy, chaplains, pastoral counselors, and other church leaders to utilize those professional skills in approaching research. Too many of us have seen research as alien to the usual ways in which we function pastorally and dialogically with those to whom we minister. Qualitative research invites us to call upon those empathic listening skills of an *I-Thou* relationship in order to listen to the lived experience of those whom we ask to participate with us as co-researchers in a qualitative research venture. In human science research with the new paradigm of varied qualitative methods, we seek to learn from the voices of the ones who are the research participants so that we may understand the nature of the directly experienced reality of those persons. Marc Briod has remarked, "As researchers we stand for the attempt to make sense of lived experience, for the importance of dwelling in and on that experience as participant-observers. We do not concede the science of human beings to the positivists or to the pure objectivists. The great American writer, Wallace Stevens, once said that `poetry is a renovation of experience.' In a different way, human science research is also a renovation of experience. And although it is far from being poetry, like poetry, it is richly descriptive and interpretive research that is of and by the heart as well as by the mind. The heart, the cultivated heart, symbolizes our embodied way of experiencing and knowing, and must be included in any full accounting of our capacity for human understanding" (1992).

Anton Boisen's famous phrase, "the living human document," is alive and well in qualitative research. While the mainstream of prior research has been around other types of documents, particularly written documents, qualitative research seeks to transfer the hermeneutical principles from scriptural studies to the understanding and the interpretation of the experiences of the *living human* document. Out of the information-rich experiences of the participants in qualitative research, the investigator seeks to discover the meanings and to make the interpretations that are congruent with the perceptions of the co-researchers. In numerous ways, the utilization of qualitative research methodology provides the pastoral caregiver with a natural bridge from the practice of ministry to the understanding and meanings of that ministry to persons.

## PASTORAL RESEARCH PROBLEMS
## WITH A QUALITATIVE DESIGN

The array of research problems related to the pastoral arts which have proved naturally suited to a qualitative methodology is fascinating. These studies have a strong connection with pastoral care and counseling, and it is important to note how similar research projects could develop out of your daily ministry. These projects have all sought to listen and then to interpret and articulate the experiences of persons who have gone through some painful or stressful life events: (1) Young adults who had lost a parent between the ages of 7 and 17 were interviewed for their reflections on their lived experience of what it was like to be a child coping with the death of a parent. The type of death (suicide being the most difficult), the suddenness of death or length of sickness, the nature of the child's support system following death, the overall impact on the person's development of that tragedy, and other issues and themes that emerged from the research gave many clues to the type and quality of ministry that would be helpful to children under those circumstances. (2) Since there has been almost no research of any kind done on long-term sobriety of alcoholics and the place of spirituality in that sobriety, a design was set up to interview male alcoholics who started their recovery journey with AA and who had achieved at least 10 years of sobriety. Many things were discovered from eliciting the knowledge and experience of these men that is helpful for pastors in working with alcoholics and their recovery. (3) One study explored the perceived influence of women religious in the Roman Catholic tradition on their personal adult identity from the experience of living in a religious community. (4) Child abuse has been investigated in terms of its impact on the conscious mental representatives of God. Various research projects have used qualitative methodology to explore how various traumas from violence have impacted the perceived mental representations of God. (5) The voices of immigrants, ethnic groups, and the marginalized have been the center of human science research projects so that the experience of those persons can be better understood and the care given to those persons can be more relevant to the needs and the problems elicited from the research interviews. (6) The experience of forgiveness in the lives of selected groups of research participants, such as from abusive families, has served to inform the ministry of helping and healing through forgiveness for those people. (7) Therapists' inattention to female clients' experiences of stillbirth or miscarriage, as well as collusion with the denial of the grief process, have been highlighted by a qualitative study which interviewed female clients who had experienced such a loss. In that study, only one therapist, who incidentally was a pastoral counselor, utilized any healing and therapeutic ritual with a client. Most therapists ignored the significance in the women's lives of such a traumatic loss. (8) In addressing the question of the importance of personal therapy for a psychotherapist or pastoral counselor, a qualitative study clarified the mixed findings from numerous quantitative studies. Some studies came up with positive findings indicating support for therapists having their own personal therapy or didactic analysis. The other half of the studies had negative results and indicated that personal therapy for psychotherapists was not helpful. The qualitative study zeroed in on the depth experience of a dozen therapists, some of whom had had some poor experiences in their personal therapy. But the therapists were unanimous in affirming the value of personal therapy for therapists, including the fact that they had learned much about what not to do from some of the unhelpful things that they had experienced in their own therapy.

## HISTORICAL AND PHILOSOPHICAL FOUNDATIONS

The historical and philosophical underpinnings of qualitative research constitute a rich and varied story. Names such as Schleiermacher, Dilthey, Husserl, Heidegger, Gadamer, Habermas, Buber, Giorgi, and Polkinghorne are woven into the history and philosophy of qualitative research. These people and their philosophical perspectives challenged the norms of natural science as the only approach to research in the human sciences, but the details of that intellectual journey are best read in other places (Barbaria, 1993; Reinharz, 1992; Strauss & Corbin, 1990; Taylor & Bogdan, 1984). For our purposes, the most significant factor is Buber's *I-Thou* relationship of mutual respect between the researcher and the research participant(s) which provides an undergirding context for qualitative research in the process of seeking to listen to the lived experiences of persons. Feminist and liberation theological perspectives, which challenge all of us to listen to the voices of the oppressed, the marginalized, and the disempowered, have been supportive of the efforts of qualitative research to understand and to interpret the "different" voices of the world. In fact, in some instances qualitative research has taken on a prophetic task in at least two ways. Qualitative research has challenged ethnocentric, Euro-American, left-brained, male-dominated ways of thinking about science, the sources of knowledge, and the appropriate methods of human research. It has also been used as the basis for structuring social programs to address the problems of the oppressed and dispossessed, whose voices have been heard in the process of qualitative research studies conducted among them.

A comparison of the underlying principles of qualitative research with those of quantitative research may help to clarify the significant difference in the new paradigm of qualitative research. Lynda Mainwaring (1991) summarizes the different assumptions of the two paradigms in the following way:

I. Logical positivism, which undergirds quantitative research:
   a. Reality can be objectively determined by empirical observation,
   b. Causality is linearly determined,
   c. The hypothethico-deductive system of theory testing can lead to theory verification or disconfirmation,
   d. Generalization can be established through induction.

II. Qualitative research:
   a. With respect to causality, "any observed action is the instantaneous resolution of a large number of mutual, simultaneous shapers, each of which is constantly shaping, and being shaped by, all other shapers" (Guba & Lincoln, 1989, p. 106).
   b. Individuals describe reality by reference to their conclusions and these are based on the structure and function of mentation.
   c. Investigators and research participant are active agents.
   d. The observer and the observed impact upon one another.
   e. Investigations, including scientific investigations, are value-laden.
   f. Meaning is a social, linguistic, historical, cultural, and contextual product.

While the implications of these differences will be spelled out in the following chapters, it is important to appreciate that qualitative research is seeking to open up other avenues to explore the life experiences of human beings in an inclusive manner.

# 9 | Initial Principles and Disciplines

**B**efore plunging into a consideration of qualitative research, you may want to ask what kind of qualitative method—ethnography, grounded theory, phenomenology—will be presented here. In the spirit of qualitative thinking, it is important that you, the reader, be fully informed about the perspective the writer presents.

The qualitative method presented here is "generic" rather than specific to any one school. Because I (HB) came to the movement early in the 1970s, I was not trained in any specific method. Following my theological studies and grounding in existentialism, my doctoral dissertation required me to articulate the methodology of Martin Buber, which in turn led me to immerse myself in the seminal qualitative work of his teacher, Wilhelm Dilthey. Dilthey, writing at the turn of the century, founded a qualitative method for all human sciences prior to the birth of phenomenology or any of its particular methods.

When I began teaching qualitative research methods, my students and I reviewed the authors articulating this method in each of the social sciences and found that there was no established way of doing qualitative research in any one of the social sciences. Rather, the specific method of each author was shaped *in situ* by his or her research interests and experiences. Phenomenology, for example, is a philosophy, not a social science method, and its specific adaptations to the social sciences differ from author to author.

On the other hand, I also found that there were basic, commonly held principles and strategies not only within each social science, but across all of them. Despite the preferences of some for more structure and others for more free responsiveness, shaped by the needs of their research problems (and their reactions to a quantitative approach), there was a concordance among all about the values and procedures of a method generically called "qualitative." While I found a fundamental demarcation between all of these methods and quantitative methods and values, I found no essential contradictions between one qualitative methodologist and another. Vocabulary differed, accentuations differed, but the meanings and methods were comparable. This is striking when you consider that each of the social sciences and authors was responding to their individual quest for discovery and understanding and that they seldom if ever referred to each other's methods.

In a sentence, the method presented here is generic, not purist in any one articulation. Moreover, I believe that qualitative methodology is quite young and still in the process of discovering its full power as a method and that any "established," conformist procedure will destroy the spirit and power of qualitative research. Only by striving to discover and understand each human experience, and by using any approach which best enables an individual researcher to accomplish this, does a qualitative approach remain "pure." Closing this preface on the author of this chapter, let me now turn to you, the researcher.

### The Instrument

The instrument used in qualitative research to gather and interpret material is *you*, the researcher. You are the instrument through which the other's experience is engaged, meaning is discovered, and a verbal representation made to your audience. If statistical research utilizes various objective instruments— T-tests, ANOVA, and other mathematical formulas—and works to minimize the contaminating influence of the researcher, then the qualitative method embraces the researcher as its principal, even sole, instrument. This is not by preference but due to the intrinsic nature of the qualitative method: only the human mind can "read" human expressions and grasp meaning.

For this reason, we need to begin examining this methodology by focusing on you, the researcher. How does a qualitative researcher think? How can this thinking pattern be enhanced and given rigor? How does the researcher manage his or her involvement? How can the quality of the intervention be disciplined and improved? What stumbling blocks must be avoided?

### Being Clear About the Differences in Methods

A first step is to be clear about the differences between qualitative and quantitative norms and not mistakenly design one type of research project by the criteria of the other. Both are powerful methods for finding truth, but each has its own unique logic and its own path to follow, each finds a different kind of "truth," and each has its own criteria for excellence of process. Your research will be quite diminished in quality and credibility if, unwittingly, you design it mixing quantitative norms with qualitative ones.

In many ways, the criteria of excellence in qualitative research are just the opposite of those of quantitative research. In terms of its objective, the qualitative approach does not intend to test, prove, persuade, or argue a particular predetermined point, and it would be inappropriate to use it for any of those purposes. Its purpose is to discover the meaning of a human experience and to communicate this understanding to the reader. It does this through narrative rather than through numbers, with the understanding that its narrative words evoke the human experience attached to them. This narrative description, as all human communication, can only approximate the human experience. Qualitative research can never offer "facts" or *the* reality, but only a relatively faithful analogy of what the human experience means to the participant.

To accomplish its mission, the qualitative approach must *engage* or participate in the experience rather than remain outside of or objective with respect to it. In the engagement, rapport and trust, not control and manipulation are essential. Understanding comes contextually and as a whole, rather than by isolating each element and analyzing it in isolation. The quality of this engagement is measured in terms of "depth of involvement," not in terms of "how many." If relevant at all, large numbers diminish the quality of this method rather than enhance it and, on the other hand, a case study of one individual can be quite fruitful.

Two final norms must be explained at more length. One is that the perspective ("bias") of the researcher is dealt with by openly acknowledging it and working with it, rather than by attempting to eradicate it or control for it mathematically. The other is that the qualitative process is circular rather than preset and linear. The researcher continually selects his or her next step out of new learnings and the unanticipated options that arise as each step of the research process unfolds. Predefinition diminishes the possibility of discovery.

In many ways, qualitative norms are the opposite of those we are accustomed to in quantitative approaches. To utilize this method competently, we need to be conscious of its unique logic and apply it consistently.

### How a Qualitative Researcher Thinks

Qualitative research has a unique manner of thinking and discovery in its research process, one which can best be described as "dialogical." This dialogue is engaged in continuously, both on the intrapersonal, thinking level, and on the interpersonal, research/subject level. We will begin here by describing the dialogical nature of the internal thinking level.

Qualitative work requires an unusual discipline of thinking, including but expanding beyond the logical, problem-solving skills ordinarily taught in academia. Here thinking is bicameral, utilizing our intuitive, creative thinking patterns as well as our rational ones, and then adding a dynamic interplay between the two. The discipline is demanding, yet merely refines and directs the way we think in everyday life.

We are well aware of our *rational* thinking skills, the thinking processes we are conscious of, have control over, and follow step-by-step. We are given a problem. We consider what we know and what we want to know. We break it down into its individual elements and consider each, one after the other, moving from one element and connecting it to the next. In a line of logic, we work our way down the line to the problem's solution. Whether we work logically with clear and distinct concepts or whether we work mathematically with formulas, the process in our minds is systematically directed by us. Ordinarily, this is what we mean when we say we are "thinking."

But there is another modality in the mind, another kind of thinking we engage in continuously. Some call it *intuitive* thinking, some "creative" thinking. Most of us are oblivious to its activity because its leading characteristic is that we are not reflectively conscious of it. We are not aware of the thinking process but only of the product. Without our awareness, our five senses inundate our mind at every moment, reporting millions of elements of data from the outside world. This intuitive (some call it *gestalt*) mind receives and organizes these multitudinous fragments of sense experience into a single, whole picture, selecting an organizing focal point laying out all the other elements around it in its related context. This mental organization discloses a unifying form and gives us a meaningful interpretation of the experience reported in fragments by the senses.

Our intuitive mind cannot tolerate fragmentation; it seems impelled to discover a whole, a pattern and significance in whatever we experience. And when it completes its form-identifying task, this resulting figure/ground organization is then transferred across to our conscious, rational mind where the mental picture is given a representative name, a verbal handle, signifying this interpretation.

While we are not consciously aware of this thinking process but only of the name identifying the result, we are aware, through our feelings, that this thinking process is taking place. You can observe this in yourself through the following exercise. Keep one eye on your emotional experience as you engage this cognitive task. Turn the page and look at *Figure A*. What do you see?

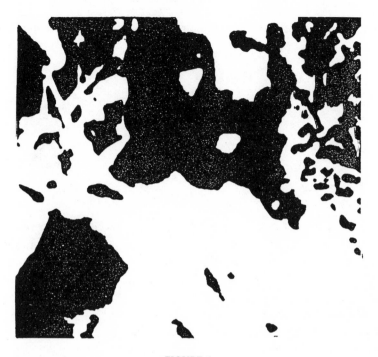

FIGURE A

Initially, if your experience is similar to others, you will feel yourself uneasy, disquieted, even annoyed as you struggle to make sense of this picture. Your intuitive mind is working away at the picture but not able to make sense of it. If a resolution does not come early, your mind will want to turn away to relieve the tension, but somehow it does not like to let go of the unresolved. Then there is that "a ha!" of euphoric release as your mind recognizes a whole and is able to name it. "It's a bearded prophet in a white robe!" And with the naming comes a resolution and a release which allows your intuitive mind to enjoy its success and then to turn its attention to something else.

The Gestalt Psychologists have identified some interesting characteristics of how the intuitive part of our mind thinks, characteristics which form the foundation of our qualitative discipline. While it will require a bit of patience, allow me to describe several of these characteristics.

*Form characteristics.* The first is that the intuitive mind looks for a *form* which can organize the elements rather than looking at the elements themselves. Whether we call it the essence, paradigm, significance, gestalt, theory, structure, meaning, or whatever, it is a unifying form. The Gestalt Psychologists called it the *Gestalt-Qualität*, "the something more than the sum of the parts."

In *Figures* B and C, the form "triangle" unifies both the three lines in B and the set of seemingly unconnected lines and areas in C.

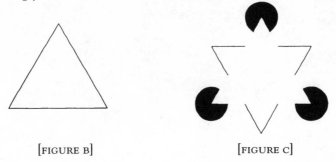

[FIGURE B]                    [FIGURE C]

In a process that is more systemic than logical, more interdependent than linear, the mind selects one element which becomes the foreground or focal point of the form, and allows the rest to make up the background or supporting context. Note that in B it selects the black lines as the foreground, while in C the white space becomes the foreground. Note also that in both figures the context or background is as important as is the focus in giving us meaning; without their interdependence, there can be no meaning.

The intuitive mind is relentless in its endeavor to find a form. In what is described as the hermeneutic circle, it moves from the whole to each element and simultaneously from each element to the whole. And since a throng of elements could support various forms, the intuitive mind will elect that form which is the simplest, clearest, and most appropriate to interpret this mass of data. It shies away from complexity. *Figure D* is simply a "cube" rather than "three sets of four parallel lines, horizontal, vertical, and diagonal." The simpler form usually is also the more dynamic, insightful, and memorable.

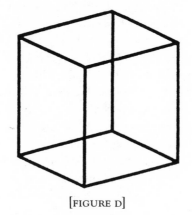

[FIGURE D]

In Figure E the central item is either a letter or a number, depending on the context the mind elects.

$$12$$

$$A \; 13 \; C$$

$$14$$

[FIGURE E]

Once a successful form is selected, the intuitive mind becomes satisfied and loses interest, as it were, moving on to the next puzzle of data. The nominated form itself tends to become fixed in our mind; the gestalt mind is reluctant to look again and see if there is another way to interpret the data. This is easily demonstrated with the familiar young girl/old hag drawing of *Figure F*. Whichever image we identify first, we find it difficult to "let go" and find the other image.

[FIGURE F]

Closure is another important intuitive process for the qualitative researcher. Sense data seldom supplies all the pieces needed to create a complete gestalt; usually some are missing. To complete the form, these missing elements are supplied from our memory of our own past experiences. While *Figure G* is a simplistic example of closure, the role of this phenomenon will be involved on a more complex level in the qualitative research process.

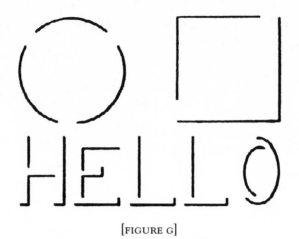

[FIGURE G]

These rather simple examples, demonstrating how the intuitive mind thinks in its own unique manner, are analogous to how it thinks in the multifarious experiences of everyday life. Although the sense elements which are fed into the intuitive mind are more complex, the process of organizing and interpreting them into meaning remains the same. Since the thinking of our intuitive mind is so commonly ignored, and yet is basic to qualitative thinking, the task here is to give you some awareness of these processes. Once you become conscious of how the intuitive mind works, you will be in a position to discipline it and increase its effectiveness.

For example, we noted that a form requires both a focus and a context; meaning cannot exist without the interdependence of the two. Yet our rational mind tends to name only the focal point and leave the context as unidentified and taken for granted. Unfortunately, in a human experience, all the emotional, more "human," dynamic, and colorful elements of the experience fall within this contextual area. For the qualitative researcher to gain and communicate understanding, he or she must expand his or her consciousness and become *fully* aware of the experience—focus and context together—and not identify the focal point only. Both need to be carefully articulated in the researcher's notes. And if an understanding of this human experience is to be re-created in the minds of an audience, both the focal point and its defining context need to be verbally transferred in the research report.

*Interdependence.* Between these two modes of thinking, intuitive and rational, there is an interdependence which can also be described as a dialogue. The workings of each depend upon the complementary work of the other. The intuitive mind's forms cannot be consciously "held" until they are transferred to and verbally named by the rational mind. On the other hand, the rational mind only holds these names as a set of keys; the full meaning, the expansive experiential impact of these names, remains in the intuitive mind. When the name given by the rational mind is enunciated, it refers to and awakens all that human experience lying behind it in the intuitive mind.

The word *love* of itself means little. It is the prior human experience of love in each of us, called to empathic awareness of the word *love*, that enables the two of us to communicate with each other this profound human experience.

This dialogue between these two modes of our human mind provides another basis for articulating the skills needed to engage the qualitative method. Between the two is a natural cycle of discovery. Initially, the intuitive mind takes in and is "loaded up" with experience. During this phase, the mind abandons itself to the engagement of the experience and receives all the elements which the senses present to it. Then comes an incubation phase in which the intuitive mind goes to work and forms a gestalt out of all these elements while the researcher attends to other, less involving activities, or simply experiences a dry period. The third phase is the "a ha!" in which the rational mind receives and identifies the form and the emotions experience a bit of euphoric energy. In the final phase, crucial to the creative cycle, the researcher articulates in words and rational terms, as completely as possible, the contents and insights of the new form.

When he or she knows the flow of this cycle, the researcher's discovery process can become more focused. In the first phase, one can abandon oneself totally into the present experience rather than holding on to the security of previous definitions. The researcher can also learn to endure the ambiguity of the undefined experience longer, more confidently, without prematurely rushing to the surface for the security of a defining name.

Understanding the incubation phase allows the researcher to be patient and nurture this unconscious thinking process rather than forcing a premature, rationally made definition or becoming anxious about apparent writing blocks. And obviously, while the spontaneous and euphoric discovery phase is enjoyed by all, the careful work of articulating this discovery in the final phase cannot be neglected. This final task takes some of the wind out of the sails of our imaginative euphoria, but to shortchange it compromises our quest for understanding.

This brings us to the second characteristic of the intuitive/rational dialogue: the descending cycle into the depth of insight. Probably the hardest yet most beneficial discipline comes when the researcher suspends hard-earned definitions at the end of the creative cycle and returns, seemingly tabula rasa, to the beginning of the cycle all over again. Without this conscious discipline, the intuitive/rational mind prefers to be satisfied with its initially identified meaning, to be finished with this experience and move on to the next. It takes an intentional determination to both suspend your present interpretation and to reenter the exploratory cycle.

One phenomenologist describes the process as "surrender and catch," in the image of a boy throwing a ball against a wall, then stepping back, waiting, and catching it again, just to repeat the sequence of activity all over again. The qualitative researcher engages human experience with full participation, steps back and catches the mind's verbal understanding of that experience, and then lets go of articulation and returns once more to self-immersion in the experience. *In each round, the understanding of that experience becomes deeper, more empathic, more insightful.* True, there is a point which Glaser and Strauss (1967) call "theoretic saturation" when the researcher conceives a level of understanding that will not be surpassed. But this is well beyond the first interview or the first day of participation in the setting. This research process, the disciplining of the mind's dialogue between its intuitive and rational modes, is to be carefully practiced and nurtured by the qualitative researcher.

## How a Qualitative Researcher Engages

As has been noted, the dialogue takes place on two levels—internally between the two modes of the mind and externally between researcher and subjects. We turn our attention now to this second, *I-Thou* level of dialogue. A fascinating difference between quantitative and qualitative research occurs at this level. In quantitative approaches, the researcher remains outside and separate from the object under research, and the object is considered inert and determined—a "thing" to be acted upon and manipulated. In qualitative approaches, the researcher is inside the research activity, personally engaging, while the "object" of the research activity is also a human personality, free, intelligent, and also personally engaging. The two work together in the discovery process on a level of mutual dependence and trust.

*Co-researcher.* In looking first at the *Thou* side of the *I-Thou* dialogue, let us consider the qualitative researcher's view of what we ordinarily call the "subjects" of the research project. This is the name given to them by the quantitative tradition, but since quantitative terms subtly misguide the process, many writers prefer to call them "participants" or "co-researchers."

These are the individuals who have experienced the phenomenon the researcher wishes to understand. On the one hand, they are intelligent, usually quite verbal, and reflective individuals who are willing to have an open, trusting relationship with the researcher. In most cases, they are equally interested in and anxious to understand the phenomenon under investigation. On the other hand, the phenomenon usually rests within them, more as a lived experience than as a reflected one. Prior to the researcher's engagement, they have not carefully reflected upon, analyzed, or articulated the experience in rational detail. Their participation in the process of co-discovery has the character of spontaneous storytelling and free association, and the activities of reflection and meaning-searching occur between the co-researcher and researcher during their engagement. Under the guidance of the researcher's questions and curiosities, the co-researcher reflects, remembers, and attempts to put into words the dynamics and dimensions of a particular life experience. In this cooperative manner, the two discover together.

Of course, there are exceptions to this level of immediate cooperation. When the researcher is working with children, or studying materials such as pictures or letters, or doing participant-observation in a strange setting, this dialogue, while engaged, is not as direct. Nevertheless, even here the help of significant informants may be sought: parents and professional helpers of children, the creators or confidants of the letterwriter or artist, "bi-cultural" members of the new setting who can "translate" and dialogue about the setting's customs and meanings. In some manner, the co-researcher's pole of the dialogue must be given voice.

*Researcher.* Turning now to the *I* pole of the *I-Thou* dialogue, we consider the researcher's own voice. In logical terms, his or her role may seem paradoxical, yet it compares to many other human experiences, particularly to the helping professions. To paraphrase Dilthey, the researcher understands the participant's Thou through his or her own I, understands the other's experience through his or her own life experience, yet does not confuse the two. He or she is able to understand and describe the other's experience as uniquely that of the other. Obviously, this requires maturity, experience and self-discipline on the part of the researcher.

The first discipline is for the researcher to know him- or herself in regard to his or her quest and, on the essentials related to this quest, to share this self-awareness with the reader. Being inside the research activity, he or she is as much an influence on the knowledge discovered as are the co-researchers. The final interpretation is first engaged through the perspective, filtered and synthesized through the mind, and articulated in the words of the researcher. Given this level of involvement, the appropriate response on the part of the researcher is not to deny or conceal this influence, but rather to raise it, as fully as possible, to the level of reflected consciousness, and to disclose it to the reader.

The researcher must have a perspective, must look at the phenomenon from some particular vantage point, for he or she cannot be ubiquitous and cannot be objectively non-present. If you are to observe the room you are in, you can sit where you are now, go to a corner, or even stand outside the window, but you have to look at it from some vantage point, and you will observe it from that limited perspective. And this particular perspective exists on many levels. You will be very much a participant who has had similar experiences or an observer who is relatively naive to this experience. You will think and see it as a psychologist or anthropologist or theologian. Your gender, age, and cultural background will all significantly influence your engagement and understanding. While you cannot engage and understand the phenomenon except from a particular perspective, that limiting point of engagement needs to be raised to awareness and taken into account. The *I* of the dialogue needs to be clearly and openly identified.

Following this consciousness-raising effort comes the logically contradictory task of bracketing: suspending your own predispositions and intentionally opening yourself up as fully as possible to all the presentations and uniqueness of the other. Parallel to the mental discipline of letting go of your first articulated discovery and reengaging the creative cycle, so as a researcher you must first articulate, then suspend your point of view to more fully discover the object of research in all its uniqueness and refinement of presentation.

This is the paradox: the researcher needs to know his or her own ground and be rooted in it, and at the very same time, to suspend that ground and go out to the co-researcher as openly and fully as possible, fully immersing the self in the engagement. Admitting to its logical contradiction, I am assuming that most of my readers, being helping professionals themselves, will understand the meaning of this *I-Thou* engagement.

Two observations are necessary to clarify the researcher's discipline. First, recall the *closure* factor. In our efforts to understand another's experience, we fill in from our own past experience any incomplete elements in our communication with the other—and we do this unconsciously. This is what we call *bias*. To the degree we can become aware of our own experience, we bring this tendency under control and reduce our bias. But there are limits to this effort. We can never know or identify all of the biasing influences of our culture nor of all the layers of life-experience which have shaped our personality. We do what we can; there are no absolutes in qualitative research, only an open honesty and fidelity to the effort.

Another observation is that this process of raising the researcher's consciousness of the I's influence continues throughout the process. As the researcher engages the experience of the co-researcher in depth, he or she will, at the same time, become more and more aware of him- or herself, identifying with and distinguishing from the experience of the participant. Each engagement requires stepping back and articulating, not only the self and experience of the other as best it has been understood, but also a clarification of the researcher's own ground as distinct from her or his discovery. This cyclical discipline not only does not distract but actually intensifies the researcher's insight into the phenomenon under study.

There is another role for the researcher in this dialogue that bears consideration: the responsibility to continually make critical choices in the direction of the research as the process unfolds. Since this is a discovery process, and little can be anticipated beforehand, the investigator is continually faced with a multiplicity of choices at each stage of the process, each one of which will influence the outcome of the study. What setting and which set of co-researchers will be the focus? In what direction will the number of participants be expanded, and at what point will the researcher say "enough"? How will notes be collected and stabilized? How can the material best be analyzed? The investigator makes and modifies these choices based on intuitions of the situation and knowledge and expertise acquired at particular points in the process. Qualitative work is circular and iterative, rather than preset and linear, continually bending back on itself and modifying both its understandings and its direction. All this is the responsibility of the researcher, who alone can make these choices and methodological decisions.

The dialogical nature of the discovery experience usually expands beyond the researcher and co-researchers, adding to the depth and enrichment of the discovery. Frequently the researcher will enlist the aid of colleagues to read over the materials and transcripts and discuss together the meanings imbedded in them. Such discussions clarify the themes and expand the researcher's awareness of the various facets of the experience. When the first interpretation is completed, the researcher can invite a group to come and discuss the interpretation together. Sometimes these are the co-researchers of the study, sometimes other subjects who have had the same experience, sometimes a group of experts. While corrections and disconfirmations can be made at this meeting, the conversation typically is quite animated and not only confirms the original interpretation but opens new doors and gives it greater depth.

The mission of this chapter has been to give you a feeling for the logic of the qualitative process on the level of practice, to let you see its involved personal and interpersonal style. In its undulation through abandoned engagement, followed by withdrawal and articulation, and a return to a renewed immersion in an ever-deepening gyre, the method has a logic and a discipline. These offer the researcher and readers a greater depth of discovery and a clearer understanding of the human experience. From here, we move to the initial, preparatory steps to be taken in this discovery process.

# 10

# Preparations

**Q**ualitative work is exciting and energizing, and once your interest about a human experience has been aroused, you will want to begin immediately to pursue it. However, before you begin engaging people and gathering your material, three preliminary steps should be taken: clearly define your focus, develop a theoretical context, and lay out a plan of research. If your research is for a grant or an academic paper, these three steps will be required as a proposal. If your research is for your own professional learning only, these preparations will increase the power and success of your study significantly.

*Worksheets*

The very first step for engaging in a qualitative research project is to select a notebook in which you can capture your thoughts as they occur and in which you can gradually construct your study. Divide the notebook, side-by-side, into two sections, one for information, observations, and descriptions as they are met, and the other for your thoughts, insights, and interpretations as they occur to you in reference to the material on the first side and your research question as a whole. There are many ways of doing this, but most obvious is to use the right page of a notebook for description and the left for interpretation. This design will support the back-and-forth dialogical nature of your process.

Recognize from the beginning the interactive process of qualitative research. Here and in all how-to methods books, the steps will be presented one after the other in linear fashion. An orderly, intelligible presentation requires this. But in reality, the process is quite circular and interlocking. You will be continually thinking back, clarifying and revising one phase while you are engaging another. You will be analyzing your material while you are gathering it. You will rethink your literature as you engage your field. Thoughts of how you will interpret the experience will occur throughout, and you will still be refining your basic research question as you complete your study. One step sheds light and clarification on a previous step.

The important advice here is that, from the beginning, you capture and support all these reflections and mental conversations by putting them down on paper. "Objectivizing" your thoughts by writing them out supports and intensifies the discovery process.

Some authors have also found it helpful to keep a third set of notes on their methods process. Within it, they record their initial plan and anticipations, then the various impacting or unanticipated events and interactions which occur on the way, and their responses to these, and finally their revision of plans and rationale for these new choices.

### Preparation One: The Focal Question

Your first task is to identify and refine the focal question: What human experience do you wish to discover and understand? A research method follows the research question; a method is only a tool and you select the appropriate tool for the type of question you want answered. Qualitative methodology is an inappropriate tool for persuasion or for testing. Quantitative method is the right tool for taking a hypothesis and testing it to see if it is scientifically true. Theoretical research is the tool of choice for arguing logically to persuade the reader of the validity of a particular idea. But when the qualitative method is used to persuade the reader to adopt an idea the researcher has already predetermined, we have indoctrination, not research. Correctly used, this tool is limited to the discovery, description, and interpretation of a human experience engaged through an interpersonal exchange. The focal question, then, identifies a human experience the researcher wishes to understand.

May a researcher select an experience with which they have had some personal involvement, or should it be a topic about which they are totally naive? A qualitative stance recognizes that the researcher always has some subjective connection to the topic, if only curiosity, and that there are pluses and minuses to this relationship, whatever it might be. If the researcher is a close participant in the topic, i.e. has lost a sibling by suicide or is the teacher in the classroom he or she wishes to qualitatively evaluate, he or she has the advantage of an intimate understanding of the other's experience, a sensitivity the outsider will not have. The disadvantage is that, in being so close, much of the experience has become habituated, taken for granted, and much of its communication is no longer consciously noticed. The investigator does not see the experience as if for the first time and will need to do intense work to separate his or her own experience from that of the participants.

On the other hand, if the researcher is an outsider, naive to the experience, who has never lost a sibling or has never taught in a classroom, he or she has the advantage of seeing everything, every expression that communicates the experience, sharply as if for the first time. While being a keen observer, the researcher will have no "map" of understanding in which to interpret these expressions. He or she may have no awareness of their meaning, of which are significant and which are trivial, and will need to work intensely to gain a sensitive understanding of the nuances of this experience.

Every researcher stands on a line extending from being a full participant to being a total stranger to the experience under investigation. Neither extension on the continuum is preferable, for each offers strengths and weaknesses to the research. The researcher's task is to own and bracket his or her advantages and, on the other hand, to find ways to shore up and compensate for his or her blind side.

One qualification needs to be added to this advice. If the researcher is a participant in the experience but has not yet resolved that experience internally, he or she will not be able to discover it in others. If he or she has lost a sibling by suicide, for example, and has not yet completed the process of grieving and adjustment, the research project cannot be used to resolve the process.

At this early point in your project, your goal is to be able to write up your quest in one sentence. Make your focus as pointed and clear as possible, including its limiting elements. Rather than studying anxiety, you will study the anxiety of eight male graduate students experienced during their doctoral dissertations. The qualitative method is more effective when it focuses on a limited, specific event than when it looks at a broad, relatively undefined experience. Focus leads to greater depth and to the discovery of the universal element within this particular instance. Broader approaches overwhelm the researcher with a multiplicity of details and possibilities of interpretation; depth of insight is lost.

## Writing Out Your Research Quest

Articulating your research quest in writing requires you to address two more topics. After the specific statement of your *focal question* comes its full *explication*, followed by a statement of *motivation*.

The *explication* (sometimes called rationale or background or one of many other similar terms) accompanies your one sentence research statement and provides the reader with an intellectual background in terms of which to understand this tightly abstracted statement. Recall our principle that understanding requires a context. The statement by itself conceptually informs your readers, but without further elaboration, it requires them to project, out of their own backgrounds, much of what they think you intend in this study. The statement cannot be fully understood unless a developed context accompanies it.

This elaborating frame can take the form of stating a series of subquestions; giving a history of the problem; placing it within the conversation of an academic or clinical field, or subfield; unfolding and explaining the terms of the focal question; or describing previous research in this area and its limits. Each focal question offers many possibilities for such a contextual setting and the problem is to make a limited selection, enough to do the job of framing it but not burying it with complexity. Because your own extended involvement can cause you to lose touch with what is clear and what remains obscure about your question, it is recommended that you get the help of naive friends to read over your material and then ask them what they think you intend from what you have written.

The third topic to be articulated is the *motivation* for this study (sometimes called significance or justification). There may be several motivations which lead you and your readers to engage this topic. One of them can be the personal reasons which initially struck an interest in you, the researcher, but several others can point out how this new understanding can benefit your colleagues in the field, whether they be academics or clinicians. At this early stage in the use of a qualitative approach, these reasons can often include the observations, as yet there exists little or no research in this area, that there is little understanding of the experience from the co-researcher's perspective, that our clinical response to this experience requires a better understanding of all its dynamics, or that, for all of our research, the problem persists as much as ever.

If your research effort is being developed for a formal report, such as a dissertation or a research grant, this three-part articulation process will form your first chapter or section, because the articulation will be required for that report. But required or not, the articulation is an intrinsic part of the research process. It is undertaken primarily for you and your research interests, and only secondarily to fulfill the institutional requirement as well.

*Preparation Two: Literature*

The use of a literature section in the qualitative research process is still problematic and in need of definition. Some authors, Clark Moustaskas (1990) for example, argue against its use, saying that it predefines the researcher and biases any discovery. Most others assume its presence but say little about its content, role, or value in the overall research effort. Used intentionally, however, a literature study can provide the positive benefits of adding intensity and depth to the study, increasing its focus, sensitizing the researcher to subtleties of the phenomenon, making available a set of refined descriptive terms, and providing a particular professional conversation in which to communicate and discuss your discoveries. The down side is Moustaskas's concern that a literature study (the experience of the research community) will bias this new discovery process. His objection has some truth to it. But this bias can be managed in the same manner as that of the researcher's own previous awareness—by acknowledging and intentionally bracketing its perceptions before engaging the co-researchers and their experience. In all, there is never a "clean" path in qualitative work, only choices, and in this case, the greater gain seems to come by adding a theoretical focus. This favorable argument notwithstanding, the nature and role of the literature section remains ambiguous in the method books and leaves a lot of latitude and a few hazards for you, the researcher, to negotiate your way around. Allow me to clarify these by offering some background.

Since the qualitative method emerged under the shadow of the quantitative method, and quantitative work has a literature review preliminary to its empirical effort, we have assumed that qualitative projects should do the same. The norm for the quantitative literature review is to select several closely related studies—closely related because they used the same two or three variables proposed in the new study. They tell the reader what we already know with scientific certainty and serve as a platform from which this present study will take the next step in advancing knowledge.

However, when this same norm is applied to a qualitative literature section, many problems arise. Since qualitative topics are contextual, a given study will have *many* relevant variables, not just three or four specific ones. Moreover, these variables connected to the human experience under study are analogous value terms (e.g. *hope, trauma, social stigma, guilt*) rather than precise operational terms. Consequently, the literature pertinent to qualitative research is usually found in book-length presentations, not eight-page scientific articles, and expands across several of the social science disciplines and back over several generations—centuries—rather than the past few years. If quantitative norms are followed without extreme compromise, this preliminary literature study itself will extend through several dissertations in length.

This requires us to conclude that, if a literature section is to be included in the qualitative method, it must be redesigned to norms supporting qualitative work's own method and process. Each research must make certain choices and describe these to the reader. What follows is a review of some of the choices which need to be made.

The first necessary decision is to select a single theoretical context out of many that are relevant to the topic. This again is a matter of providing a selected conceptual background for both researcher and reader to approach the focal question. We understand contextually. For example, we can seek to discover the experiences of ambulatory disabled women, but when we place these in the context of developmental psychology of the middle-aged, or the sociology of social stigmatization, a strength and depth of perception is added that would be lost without either of these conceptual backgrounds. One is to be selected.

The next decision is whether the literature review is to be a critical study, or a conceptual overview. A critical study, as in a theoretical monograph, defines a specific parameter of literature, then analytically examines the relevant writings of each contributing author within that parameter, arguing to a particular interpretation. The conceptual overview limits itself to describing synthetically the current commanding theories and their dominant authors, the peak of scholarship on a given topic. It attempts to summarize that peak descriptively and without critical argumentation.

Given the limitations of such a chapter, and keeping in mind that it is only ancillary to and not the research study itself, the conceptual overview seems more congruent with the qualitative process. This summary chapter presents what you consider to be the cutting edge of our current expert knowledge in this conceptual area. Who are the influential authors, and what are their commanding views? How do they organize and define this topic? Do they differ on the major issues? How do they concur with each other in offering us the current scholarly comprehension of this topic?

Another choice asks us to define the role this literature will play in the overall research effort. Shall the conceptual frame serve to stimulate but not predefine the field research so that the researcher suspends definitions and begins the field work *tabula rasa*? Shall the literature be taken as a given, our best scholarly conclusions to date, and the field work of this study continue to extend our knowledge from this given? Or finally, are these two, literature and field, partners in a dialogue? Is each to present its understanding separately and then come together for a compare-and-contrast conversation at the conclusion of the study?

In summary, a literature study is helpful, but not essential to the qualitative research process. If it is chosen as an option, the researcher needs to select and describe its form and role. He or she cannot assume that a norm exists, or that the reader will recognize its nature without such a description.

*Literature Search: The How-To*

On a process level, the major concern in using a literature review is that it not be allowed to defeat the entire effort. As stated before, it is only preliminary and supportive; it should not become a mammoth burden which frustrates your real interests. Two strategies which can keep it in the first category are structure/control and mutual support.

*Structure/control.* Doing the research for the literature section requires a venture into an area which—for you—is yet undefined. You can easily lose yourself there and become overwhelmed and depressed. The first strategy, then, is to structure and define your quest so well that you continually feel emotionally in control. Heeding the discussion above will contribute to this control, guiding you to preselect the shape and definition of the literature chapter you plan to research and write. Without this plan, you could venture out with undefined assumptions which, in time, would prove to be impossible to fulfill.

An awareness of the library's structure should be added to this plan. Today's libraries have, conceptually, become two libraries. One is the computer search library, extending far beyond the walls of a particular building, and the other is the library of books and stacks housed within its four walls. Granted, these overlap, but each "library" has such a unique premise about what knowledge is and how it is to be searched that the dichotomy is worth considering. The computer search method is quick and vast and usually the first method used to develop a literature section. But computer data bases, like the quantitative literature review, are most comfortable with precise, discrete terms, with scientific research articles, and with a limited number of variables. Their collection is very horizontal, making it possible to identify almost everything ever published on a topic, but without any discrimination of quality. They are excellent for scientific information.

However, computer data bases are not adept at searching for value, for analogical terms, for the book-length development of ideas, or for contextually based, theoretical research. For this, you go to the "other" library with its reference section and its stacks. You begin, with the help of the ever-available reference librarian, by exploring the encyclopedias and other generic sources and compendiums, then working up to major authors and their significant works, and finally ending up in the stacks making fascinating discoveries never anticipated. This library is very vertical, with the capability of identifying the best and brightest, the most compelling thinkers over centuries, but limited in its ability to include everything ever published.

You will want to use both libraries, of course, but with awareness and caution. Computer searches are best done as a cooperative effort between yourself and a library staff member who has had experience with searches and the distinct vocabulary of each data base. Once you have done your computer search and identified the abstracts of a collection of articles, review them and select three to five promising articles only. Locate these and read them thoroughly, testing how relevant they are to your topic, what your understanding is after having read them, and where you think you should go from what you have learned. *Keep your own mental grounding ahead of the volume of material in front of you.*

Whether you begin with the reference library or turn to it after completing your explorations through the computer, approach it in the same manner. Explore the territory as a way of identifying the significant writings. Digest one book before selecting and expanding to others. Keep your digested notes ahead of the volume of materials you are discovering. Keep control of your exploration and discovery of this theoretical area.

*Mutual Support.* The writing of a literature section can be an isolating activity and, for some, can open the researcher to resistant or anxious feelings. Without a discourse on writers' block or procrastination, it is sufficient to advise you to plan to obtain adequate support in the form of discussion and feedback with interested friends or colleagues. This will reduce the isolation and keep you more involved in the interest and energy of your research topic than with negative writing experiences of the past.

*Preparation Three: Method Statement*

The methods section in a qualitative project has a double life. It emerges in the preparation stage as your ideal plan, and then slides into the background while the actual discovery process takes over with all its unanticipated events. Then it reemerges in the final report as a methods account, disclosing what actually took place on your research journey. Here we will describe the initial "best laid plan" version while the final version will be discussed in chapter 13.

Your preparations for your research venture become complete when you lay out a detailed plan of how you intend to go about collecting and analyzing your material. Unlike the methods chapter in a quantitative research report, this is not a rigid plan to which you are committed once it is agreed upon. In that approach, the researcher's intent is to control and manipulate the experience, while in the qualitative approach the researcher intends to respond to the experience as it unfolds and discloses itself. She or he enters the engagement with a plan, but that plan is continually modified as all the new, unanticipated discoveries and options reveal themselves. The plan is flexible and responsive.

Why have a plan at all? What purpose does it serve? This initial design facilitates your research journey. It helps clarify your focus, preview the direction your research will probably take, anticipates the various problems, decisions, and logistics you will have to deal with, and frees your mind as you engage the research experience. It addresses all the basic questions ahead of time so that, as modifications come, you will know how they will affect your overall direction.

Beyond its personal advantage to you, this initial plan performs an extended service if your project is a grant or a dissertation. It informs your overseers of the skill and care you bring to this topic by demonstrating to them your familiarity and expertise with the qualitative method and the detailed consideration you have given to each and all of the phases of the process. It strengthens their confidence in you as a researcher. Since you personally are the filter of the research, and it is you alone who will be continually modifying this plan as you go, gaining the confidence of your committee or your institution is crucial.

Such a plan might begin by informing the reader why, given your topic, you have chosen a qualitative approach, and your particular adaptation of qualitative method, as the best way to find an answer to your research question. This need not be a philosophical defense of qualitative research but only a clarification of the appropriate fit between your research question and the use of the method to satisfy that question. Follow this with a brief description of the type of qualitative technique you will employ, whether interviewing, participant-observation, documents, or a combination (this will be clarified in the next chapter).

Then, since the qualitative approach is a dialogue, you might share with the reader the perspective you bring to the discovery process—your professional/academic orientation and the degree of your involvement with or naivete about the topic. You might add the strategies you plan to use to compensate for the more limited side of your participant-observer stance; i.e. if you are more the outsider, how you plan to compensate for your lack of a native understanding, and if you are the insider, how you will regain the "first time" sensitivity of an outsider.

Unless you have already done so in your literature section, you will need to inform the reader of the role which the literature you have found is playing in your discovery process.

Move next to the setting and the other side of your dialogue, your co-researchers. If your study is participant-observation, tell the reader something of the setting and of the initial steps you need to take to gain access to the institution. If you are doing interviews, how will you identify and contact the actual interviewees? What criteria do you have for selection? How will you locate them? What will be your first contact, and what agreements or contracts will be made (e.g., informed consent)? Where and how will you meet them, and how gain rapport? What interview style do you intend to use, and what script or guideline will you use? Will there be other types of materials you will gather—group interviews, significant objects?

How will you capture the material (tape, notes) and how will you get that material into analyzable form? Will you analyze the material thematically, in stories, or case by case? Describe step-by-step your method of managing and analyzing your material, the techniques and practical steps you plan to take to code, group, or otherwise organize your material.

Finally, how do you plan to present this discovery to the reader? Will there be one or several analysis chapters? An interpretation or synthesis chapter? A commentary chapter?

This completes your plan. In general, the style of this section is descriptive, giving the details of the steps you plan to take as you work your way through your research activity, rather than persuasive, arguing or justifying your path. There may be some sharing of the reasons for major choices, but more to enable the reader to understand your direction and less to persuade him or her that your choices are "right."

Most of the options and details which you will include in your plan have not yet been discussed and will become clearer as you read on through the next two chapters on the gathering and analysis of your materials.

### Summary

There are certain preparatory steps which will contribute substantially to the power and success of your research quest: a specifically defined and clearly communicated research question, an articulated body of literature offering a contextual orientation, and a tentative plan to guide the actual research to follow. Rather than academic exercises, these are intrinsic to the dialogical process of the qualitative approach. Even when academic expectations are not present (as in commercial trade-book publishing of nonacademic qualitative studies), these preliminaries are included by the author. They require effort and seemingly impede your desire to get into the field, but in the long run, they will pay off in successful projects and more sensitive understandings of the human experience.

# 11

# Engaging the Experience

Once the preliminary preparations are completed, the qualitative effort proceeds in two phases: (1) engaging and gathering in the expressions of a human experience, and (2) employing a process of interpretation to rediscover the meaning that lies behind these gathered expressions. This chapter deals with the first phase.

The mission of the qualitative researcher is to discover the experience of another person and understand the meaning which that person accords to that experience. However, that experience and its meaning lie *inside* the other person. We cannot meet the experience directly, but only the expressions through which the other person communicates the experience. We hear the words and metaphors and stories of the co-researcher we are interviewing, and we see all the facial expressions, body language, and vocal tones that accompany his or her story. By reading all these expressions in concert, we are able to rediscover that human experience which lies behind them, along with the meaning the person has assigned to them. Phase one, therefore, of the qualitative research process is looking for the sources of these *expressions* of the human experience.

The qualitative approach divides these sources into three generic bodies: interviews, participant-observation, and documents. (The last group includes any object in which human meaning has been embedded—letters, pictures, poems.) While the three categories overlap and each can be combined with the others, they are usually presented separately by writers because of their unique characteristics and the different methods used to work with them. However, before discussing each of these sources one by one, it will help to consider them together in a brief overview.

Participant-observation is usually considered the richest or purist of the qualitative sources for several reasons. Here, the human experience is fully in the present; it is an ongoing flow in the present moment. Interviews, in contrast, actively reflect back on a past experience, and a poem, as an example of a document, is a static record of an experience now past. Moreover, participant-observation engages the human experience in its full living context, whereas interviews engage an experience removed from its context, and documents, like museum pieces, are totally decontextualized. Context is essential for human understanding.

The human experience engaged through participant-observation is a lived experience in contrast to the reflected, verbally identified experience of an interview. In the former, the meaning is latent and habituated, spontaneous and unreflected. I greet my friend by shouting his name and clasping his hand, shaking it up and down vigorously. I do not reflect on my behavior nor plan to conduct this strange ritual, let alone ponder in my mind its meaning; I just do it. And the researcher by my side cannot interrupt and ask me for an interpretation of this strange ritual without intruding upon and disrupting the experience under observation. Even then, I might not be able to explain because my behavior might have become so deeply habituated that I will have lost touch with an interpretation of its meaning. By contrast, in an interview I am reflectively verbalizing my past behavior, and the researcher is able to pursue my understanding of this ritual without disrupting the interviewing process. Since interviewing is reflective dialogue, the meaning of the human experience is much more available than it is in participant-observation.

There are, however, degrees of reflection and verbal interpretation. When speaking of history, the German language distinguishes between *Historisch* and *Geschichte*. Both are history but the former is a highly reflected, academic presentation of the past while the latter is a more spontaneous, less organized telling of the story. Interviewing, at its optimum, is *Geschichte*—personal, unprepared engagement, rich in affect and transposed context, with a fluid, emergent interpretation rather than a predefined one. In contrast, if I thoroughly reflect and abstractly theorize on the meaning of the ritual of handshaking, and I recite this prepackaged lecture to my interviewer, we do not have an interview but a monologue, a *document*.

Documents are static capsules of the past, latently embedded with human meaning. By themselves, they are the most difficult sources to work with, both because they are so completely removed from their context and because they are closed to further dialogue. Since the task is to move from the expressions of the document itself, back to the meaning intended by its creator, the researcher is highly challenged to find methods to recapture the necessary context and rediscover its intended meaning. Interestingly, one form of document research is the oldest and most highly developed type of formal qualitative methodology: the hermeneutical method used in biblical interpretation. Many of its procedures have been the basis for the development of other forms of qualitative research.

*Interviews*

Since this is the most popular method of gathering material, we will begin with interviewing methods, first describing various alternate methods and then reviewing some of the basic steps the researcher needs to take to pursue this method effectively.

Essentially, the qualitative interview is ideographic. Not only is the style of each interviewer different in the search for material, but engagement with each individual participant will modify her or his approach and make each interview different from the last. Nevertheless, there are generic patterns proposed by various authors. If we were to spread them out over a continuum, we could identify some on the right as *semistructured*, some on the left as *focused* and some in the middle as *conversational*.

In a *semistructured* interview, the researcher prepares a number of specific, open-ended questions to present uniformly to each of the participants. He or she asks each participant the first question, then listens supportively to everything the participant wishes to say in response to this question. Then, without pursuing that item further, the interviewer asks the second question, and so on. This set of questions remains the same throughout the series of interviews.

This type of interview is especially appropriate when the experience is so deeply habituated, or the participant so insecure, that this structure is necessary. It assumes that the researcher knows the general meaning of the experience and is looking for insight into each of its facets. The results of this type of interview tend to be more cognitive and informational as distinct from emotional and experiential. The major advantage of this method is the ease of its analysis; its categories are already identified by each preset question and the researcher has only to organize the material within each question. Its major disadvantage is that the researcher is imposing the basic parameters of the experience's meaning on the participant rather than discovering them from the participant.

On the other end of our continuum is the *focused* interview. Here, the researcher prepares by identifying all of his or her curiosities about the experience he or she wishes to discover, but then sets these to one side and asks the participant a single, focusing but nonbiasing question—e.g., "What is it like to be a single parent?" Then the researcher allows the participant to proceed in whatever direction and into whatever facets of the experience he or she chooses, supporting the presentation with interest, supportive remarks, and reflections of understanding, but without directive or evaluative comments. When the participant has told the story completely as desired, the researcher can then recall his or her original curiosities and see if any have not already been addressed spontaneously and fully by the participant. If not, he or she can present them one by one, asking if they too are a significant part of the experience and, if so, whether the participant can comment on them. If the participant responds to a query with some immediate recognition—"Yes, that's important!"—and proceeds to develop it, the researcher's hunch is reinforced. If a query is discounted, the investigator can become a bit doubtful.

The spirit of this method is to be totally open to discovering the experience and so to refine your curiosities as you proceed from one participant to another. If the third interview introduces a whole new, unanticipated dimension, that area would then be added to the subsequent interviews for confirmation and further elaboration. The concern is not for control and uniformity from one interview to the next, but for the discovery of the experience and its meaning as that emerges.

There are several advantages to this method. Not only do you capture the participant's story with a minimal amount of imposition, but you also capture the organization of his or her experience; how one aspect is connected to another and which facets have mental priority over the others. Also, this type of interview seems to capture more of the personal, affective qualities of the experience as well as unsuspected informational details. Its major disadvantage is the comparative difficulty of analyzing its material since each interview is so unique in its presentation.

The middle, generic type of interviewing, here called *conversational*, is gaining popularity as qualitative research moves away from the scientific concerns of objectivity and avoidance of bias, and becomes more aware of the nature of human discourse and meaning building. Among others, Elliot Mishler (1986) develops this perspective, treating the interview as a form of discourse in which the meaning of an experience is constructed jointly by the interviewer and the respondent within the conversation itself. Meaning emerges between the two, dialogically. The interviewer continually reformulates the questions in light of the respondent's answers and the respondent continually reframes the answers in terms understood by the interviewer. Both work together to more accurately and more fully articulate the experience of the respondent for their mutual understanding.

This type of interview has the advantage of giving the participant the support and engagement that the focused interview lacks without imposing the confinement and predefinition of the semistructured format. It also allows the interviewer to share more of her or his own experience or naivete as the two work together for deeper discovery of the experience. The disadvantage goes back to the basic challenge of the qualitative method—much discipline is required of the interviewer to support the participant in discovering the meaning of the experience without imposing predispositions on the participant.

Bear with this repetition: These are styles of interviewing which the interviewer will draw on, but in the actual interview, they will become modified by the unique demands of the topic, the circumstances of the interview, the interviewer's personality and training, and the needs and attitude of the particular respondent. From here, we move from the alternative forms of interviewing to the procedure of engaging participants and some of the concerns which occur on the way.

The first question faced by the researcher is *who?* What criteria should be used when selecting participants? Qualitative method does not look for a sample randomly drawn and large enough to statistically represent a population. Rather, it looks for "strategic informants," individuals who have been particularly immersed in the experience yet are capable of reflecting and able to articulate that experience—mature, reflective, verbal individuals, when possible.

And as the investigator proceeds, she or he continues to balance the homogeneity or heterogeneity of the pool of participants. If the initial respondents are quite repetitious (clones of one another), then the researcher widens the criteria to more broadly represent the experience. For example, if single male parents are being interviewed, the study might be extended to men with one child or several children, to older men or younger men, to divorced men or widowers, and so on. On the other hand, if several interviews leave the researcher with unique cases and no emerging generic experience of patenting by single males, then the interviewer needs to narrow the criteria to a more homogeneous group.

How many? is usually the next question. There is no numerical answer to this since qualitative research is not concerned with numbers but with depth. The issue is one of *saturation*—when do I arrive at a gestalt, a full understanding of the experience beyond which more material gives me repetition and confirmation of my understanding, but no new facets of the experience or its meaning? There is an experience-based tradition of interviewing eight to twelve participants, but clearly multiple interviews of one person have often given the same depth as twenty separate interviews. One caveat, however, is that large numbers tend to produce less depth and lead the researcher out of the qualitative framework and into a more superficial, quasi-survey type of research.

How do I locate my participants? is the next question. Here again is a reversal of the way we have been trained to think. Since trust and rapport are essential, the paths of newspaper advertisements and random requests used in objective studies have been found to be the least successful, and word of mouth, friends of friends, the most effective. Telling others of our research interest almost invariably brings identification and suggestions for participants. Snowballing—asking each participant if he knows two other possible participants—can build on this person-to person connection.

New researchers hesitate to interview another person, aware of the time imposition and personal disclosure involved. And initially the prospective participant may be cautious. Yet the end of an interview almost invariably produces the same expressions of pleasure and appreciation by the participant. Experiencing the focused interest and effort to understand, extended over an hour or more, is an uncommon experience for most individuals. While not in therapy, it is therapeutic and appreciated. If you approach each participant out of a genuine desire to learn from him and not merely as #7 on your list, he or she will be very pleased to have been selected as a participant.

Once a potential participant is identified, or has volunteered, the interviewer makes a phone contact, explains the research interest, describes the level of involvement which will be asked of the participant, and answers any questions or concerns. After arranging a time and place to meet, the interviewer follows up with a letter, again explaining the research interest, reminding the participant of the time and place of meeting, expressing thanks in advance, and enclosing the informed consent sheet and any basic demographic questions wanted as background for the research. The informed consent statement is usually a one- or two-page signed release which again articulates the research question and gives assurance of confidentiality, anonymity, and the freedom to participate or withdraw without consequence. It should be written in clear, straightforward language rather than in legalese.

Your meeting should take place in an environment which makes your participant as comfortable and self-oriented as possible, and it should also be free of distractions and interruptions. Upon meeting your participant, make connecting with them and building rapport your primary concerns so that both of you become comfortable with each other. Your tape recorder (which should already have been cleared on the phone and in the informed consent statement) is quickly and unobtrusively set up. Explain your desire to learn everything your participant can teach you and begin the interview. When the interview is complete, ask if he or she has any concerns or comments on the interview process itself, ask if you can recontact him or her if further questions arise, and then express your thanks for this valuable contribution. A follow-up note of gratitude is always appropriate.

There are many variations of the one-to-one interview. Some researchers will interview several participants in a focus group. Excellent results have been obtained by regathering the individuals into a group after the results have been interpreted, sharing those interpretations with them, and asking them if they concur or wish to make further comments. Others will set up a comparative group to more sharply discriminate the unique characteristics of the experience, or they will select an additional foil with the opposite experience or opposite view of the experience to be added to their interview sequence. Some will select an individual case and draw on everyone who has contributed to or participated in that individual's experience, along with any materials available. Deeper human experiences are effectively probed by having a sequence of interviews with the same person and by using such various projectives to focus the conversation as time-lines, photos, sketches, or abstract drawings created by the participants.

Children and public figures are a special challenge to the interviewer's method. The latter are professionally skilled in dissembling to the media and public, presenting contrived impressions and "spins" on human situations. Children are not yet mature enough to verbalize the meaning of their experiences and require the support of other media to communicate them—puppets, doll houses, drawings—along with a lot of patience, rapport, and latitude. These and other difficult audiences are better reached through participant-observation or a combination of the three methods.

## Participant-Observation

I suspect that most readers of this book will be more apt to use interviewing methods than either participation-observation or documents. This section will nevertheless be valuable to you, not only because interviewing frequently reaches out to include some participant-observation, but also because here you can learn more of the unique approach of the qualitative method. Participation-observation is an especially valuable approach for the study of those social and cultural experiences which have become so habituated, so taken for granted, that the individual participant is incapable of reflectively articulating their meaning through interviewing. For the participant-observer, the fundamental question is: What is the socially shared meaning which makes this interaction purposeful for this group of people?

As the name indicates, the participant-observer engages the expressions of the experience by participating in them firsthand rather than by hearing about them secondhand through another participant. The name also indicates that the researcher's presence has a dual quality. He or she must be involved, immersed in the experience along with the others, but at the same time have the distance and reflection of an independent observer, no easy task. Success will be relative. No one ever does a perfect, "correct" job, but there are strategies for improving one's effort.

When entering the situation, the researcher finds him- or herself somewhere on the continuum between veteran insider and total stranger. Neither orientation is preferable; both have advantages and disadvantages. In either case, the task is to compensate for one's "shorter" side as much as possible—to stretch and strengthen one's outside observer awareness if a participant, or shore up one's inside native awareness if a stranger to the experience.

The strength of the outsider, which derives from entering the setting totally naive of any meaning, is a heightened sensitivity to all its expressions. He or she is very alert and sees everything as if for the first time. In fact, the outsider is so bombarded with all the signs, gestures, names, settings, schedules—everything—and can interpret so little of it, that the experience can become emotionally overwhelming.

To compensate for this—to begin expanding the participatory role—the researcher must either endure mystification for the days or weeks required to gain an orientation, or spend very limited amounts of time in the environment spaced by extended periods of outside reorientation used for taking extensive notes, mapping out the setting and its schedule, or focusing on one particular aspect of the experience, such as its decor (its most noticeable labels, costumes, roles, etc.). The investigator may also obtain the support of a "strategic informant," a marginal participant who can be a companion on the quest, translating the significance of all that she or he does not understand. One must especially be skilled at recording, but then setting aside all one's early interpretations. The outsider will have an intense need to create meanings and gain some security in the new setting. These early meanings are bound to be superficial and have a high degree of projection from the observer's past experiences rather than faithfully interpret the setting.

The native participant is equally blessed by an almost intuitive awareness of the meaning of every little nuance of the setting. She or he is deeply perceptive of and in communication with all the minute expressions of the environment with almost no personal projection. The difficulty is that he or she is so much a participant as to have become unaware of the expressions which communicate these meanings. The native is so oriented and perceives the environment as so established and reified that she or he has become incapable of discovering anything new or different. The distance of the outsider is lost.

As a result, researching the environment is not overwhelming, but can become boring. What his or her environment means is obvious, and, for that same reason, very difficult to put down in writing.

The participant's strategies to compensate for his or her blind side are to obtain the assistance of a co-researcher who is a total stranger to the environment and/or who will engage it from a different role or perspective. Looking for those moments in which the setting is shaken out of its normal pattern, when it is in crisis or in a celebration (the office Christmas party) will contrast, and thereby highlight, its "normal" characteristics. He or she might also try assuming a new perspective on the setting—that of a sociologist if she is a psychologist—or a new role—that of the feminist trustee if he is the conservative pastor.

No researcher is the absolute participant in a study, nor the total observer, but stands somewhere in between, favoring one polarity or the other. The researcher's task is to stretch toward both poles, to become as completely the participant and, at the same time, to enhance the naive, observer role as much as possible, in both planning and throughout the research activity.

The process of engaging in a participant-observer study is much more complicated and detailed than that of interviewing, and it begins with the first thought of the desired research topic. Note-taking begins here. Also, field research offers much less control than interviewing and there is more dialogue between what the researcher originally intends and what actually occurs. Another consideration is "gatekeeping," which refers to all those steps taken to gain entry into the environment. If it is an institution, proposals must be made, negotiations and agreements made, and permissions obtained at all levels of the organization. You begin at the top and, at each lower level, you begin anew, assuming nothing granted at the higher level. You cannot enter your environment on the authority of the "front office," but only with the good will and cooperation of those you will be working with each day.

Once you have obtained entry, you need to decide what role you will have within the environment, how you will blend in. If you take a purely observing role, you will change the environment just by your obtrusive presence "over there," observing every move and taking notes. On the other hand, you do not want to assume or be slowly pulled into a significant role because that too will modify the environment.

You must also deal with the ethical dilemma of being open in your researcher role versus being covert. The label "researcher" has an ominous meaning to some and can, in itself, neutralize your ability to learn in the setting. Ethical judgments are much more complicated for the field researcher and frequently require spontaneous decisions. Most authors follow situational ethics, balancing their dilemmas of choice toward opposing goods rather than proposing idealistic norms to be applied across the board.

Once having gotten inside the environment, your next task is to gain rapport with your fellow participants. How do you become assimilated, how can you gain their trust and openness, not only for full participation in their experience, but for informal interviews and conversations as the opportunities occur? Sometimes rapport grows gradually, but most authors report acquiring it unexpectedly through their contributions during a crisis in the setting.

Taking notes or having another method of capturing the experience and reflecting on it is another challenge. Any recording within the setting will be seen as intrusive and yet any extensive delay after the experience will result in the loss of many of your immediate impressions. Many researchers have resorted to taking their breaks in their cars or in a closet or some other convenient but private place they have been able to identify. Notes for field work experiences can become quite voluminous.

The extended research process moves into deeper and deeper interpretations of the social construction of the meaning/purpose of the setting, along with its various significant facets. As these become identified, the researcher holds them as hunches or hypotheses, and checks them out during further participation. As they become supported and firmed up, she or he experiences a saturation of understanding and diminishing return in her or his presence and research. Then it is time for the good-byes and all the amenities of appreciation for their friendships and support, but always leaving, if possible, the door open for a brief return at a later date. Once the analysis is undertaken, certain blank spots or conflicting evidence may appear and the need to "check it out" in the field will become desirable.

### Documents

Documents, also generically called artifacts, refer to any external objects which have been embedded with a human purpose or meaning. A piece of chalk is really a compressed packet of calcium, but it has been embedded with the purpose of writing upon a blackboard for classroom instruction. This specific human meaning is so impressed upon the piece of chalk that to use it for some other purpose would seem strange and out of order. And by studying the chalk stick, we can rediscover this human meaning attributed to it.

Not only do physical objects like chairs, tables, and automobiles bear this objectivized human meaning, but so also do organizations such as IBM, Brown University, and the state of Ohio. All these exist as human projections and exist only as human conventions.

The most common and most used documents in qualitative research are communication objects such as photos, pictures, letters, or poems. The recent interest in Ken Burns's *Civil War* documentary, which used photos and letters to recreate an understanding of the Civil War experience, is an excellent example of this method of qualitative research.

The greatest drawback for this source of expressions is the loss of context, which somehow must be provided. Most commonly, the documents are combined with other sources, a method qualitative researchers call *triangulation*. In psycho-biography, for example, the researcher will study the personal letters and literary writings of a subject and allow one to provide understanding of and context for the other. In addition, both will be placed in the context of the cultural and historic setting in which they were composed, realizing an even greater understanding of their meaning.

Robert Coles, using another combination, in his study, *Children of Crisis*, had children draw pictures of their home, teacher, and school. He then interviewed them using these documents to elicit and support the telling of their stories. In addition, Coles was aided in his interpretations by his participation-observation, that is by living in the environment of his children and engaging them in their own settings.

A colleague, Margaret Gendlin, studied children of divorced parents from a developmental perspective. In a public school environment, she invited these children of each grade to play with an assortment of puppets and to create a play about their parents and the divorce. Their puppet show was videotaped and then played back to them for their enjoyment and spontaneous conversation. All these sources were combined in her study in which she discovered how each age, at its level of development, understands the divorce situation of the parents and "resolves" that understanding.

Of course, the category of documents also includes written texts. As mentioned earlier in this chapter, one of the original research methods upon which qualitative methodology was founded is the science of biblical hermeneutics. A refined set of interpretive methods has been developed to discover the meaning of a biblical text and these have since been adopted, not only for the qualitative interpretation of documents, but for the entire qualitative methodology. The most famous technique is referred to as the *hermeneutic circle*, the process of interpreting the meaning of the whole through each of its parts and, as the same time the meaning of each of the parts through that of the whole.

Qualitative research is made up of two phases: (1) gathering materials, the expressions of human experience, and (2) interpreting those materials, rediscovering the meaning of the human experience which these materials express.

The next chapter takes up second phase. Conceptually, and for the purposes of a guidebook such as this, it makes sense to treat the two as distinct and sequential. In the actual practice of qualitative research, however, the two activities are very interdependent and simultaneous. The researcher cannot effectively interview without analyzing and interpreting as he or she goes, just as the insights acquired through analysis must be continuously tempered and revised in returning to interviewing. The hermeneutic circle applies to these two interdependent phases very appropriately.

# 12 | Meaning Making

Interpreting the meaning of a human experience is fundamentally a mental exercise, an activity which occurs within the human mind rather than through a mechanical external process. Meaning arises more from maturely "dwelling in" the other's experience, and expressions of that experience, than from strategies or techniques of interpretation. Nevertheless, this endeavor in a qualitative study is so enormous that the support of external strategies is essential. The techniques which I will describe in this chapter will give organization and confidence to what can be a very overwhelming effort. While they are organically intertwined, the parts of this process can be separately identified as stabilization of materials, analysis process, analysis report, synthesis report, and commentary.

## Stabilization of Materials

However you may have gathered your materials, your first need is to put your notes and experiences into a tangible, permanent, written form which you can use for your analysis. Making your impressions permanent serves several purposes. First, doing it promptly captures those all important contextual expressions, emotions, body language, and so on, before they evaporate from your mind. The words are focal in our communication and are more easily remembered. The contextual parts of the communication, however, while essential for our understanding, are only peripherally noticed (if at all) and are forgotten within the first twenty-four hours. Writing it all down shortly after the experience, separating the descriptive matter from the interpretive matter as suggested in chapter 10, captures your encounter before time and distractions wipe it from your memories.

The activity of writing it all out shortly after the experience also helps us resolve the experience in our minds. Verbalizing it brings closure and enables us to be free to concentrate and engage the next experience without having this previous event continually intruding into our thoughts and distracting us. This same verbal resolution provides us with new, more penetrating questions for our next engagement.

Finally, stabilizing the material in a permanent form allows the researcher to feel confident that the process is organized and under control, rather than feel overburdened by a multitude of unconnected items carried around in his or her head, along with concerns that this or that significant factor may be forgotten.

Should you use a tape recorder, or notes—or both? Both are recommended unless the situation limits the choice. A special value of a tape recording is that the researcher can discover the experience, both as a participant in the actual interview, and then rediscover it as an observer, listening to the tape later. These two experiences of the same interview can sometimes be strikingly different. Tapes, obviously, have an excellent memory and can capture those exact words and expressions of the participant.

The value of audiotaping, however, is often exaggerated. We think of it being a very accurate recording of the event but forget that the tape filters out almost all of the affective and visual context, parts of the experience which bring a high degree of understanding to the interviewer. And even more of this material is lost when these tapes are transcribed to typed pages. For this reason, we recommend that, in addition to an audiotaping, the interviewer take descriptive and interpretive notes to capture what the tape cannot. Since most researchers find that note-taking during the session is distracting and interferes with the total involvement of the conversation, they take their notes immediately after the meeting.

Note-taking after the fact might follow a three-layered technique. Immediately after the engagement, the researcher goes to an undistracted location and writes out the core words or ideas of the conversation and the order in which they flowed. Then she or he returns and fills in everything that can be remembered of the conversation around each of those core topics, and any others which she or he now recalls. The entire conversation is recreated and interpretive thoughts are noted. Finally, before the day ends, the researcher goes over the recording once more, adding to and annotating all the thoughts which have occurred since the first recording was written out. At first, note-taking can seem to be an unreliable method, but with a little practice, disciplined researchers find that they can recall verbatim an entire hour's interview.

Transcriptions of tapes are valuable supports to your analysis process, but they also raise a number of problems. Transcribing an hour's interview can take from six to fifteen hours of the researcher's time or, if sent out to be done by a professional transcriber, a lot of dollars. Between the two options, most prefer to do the typing themselves, even if their typing skills are only average. The work is tedious, but their transcriptions are more accurate and complete since they have a better knowledge of the conversation—these are not studio tapings—and the time and concentration spent on transcribing contributes significantly to their mind's ability to dwell in the interpretive process.

All researchers transcribe all their tapes. Some will transcribe totally those interviews which they found rich in material, then take further notes and quotations directly from the remaining tapes, others will selectively transcribe only that material which is "on topic."

Mechanical considerations need to be briefly mentioned, if only because they have so many sad stories attached to them. Use a reliable tape recorder, with new batteries and clip on, lapel microphone extensions. While the art is to make the recording as unobtrusive as possible, you will spend many hours listening to the tapes, and a minimum level of quality will make your life much easier.

### Analysis Process

The mind makes meaning out of its experiences in a holistic rather than an orderly, step-by-step manner. Once this thinking process is completed, its discovery is usually presented to the reader in the two parallel packages of analysis and synthesis (or interpretation) and then supplemented by a commentary. These four topics, process, analysis, synthesis, and commentary, can easily become confused since they are so interdependent. To minimize this confusion, I will first describe the three tangible presentations found in the report, the goals you are working toward, and then describe the thinking process and the various paths researchers use to find their way to these presentations.

### Analysis Report

This section presents the material of your research to the reader, not in the raw form of transcripts and notes, but in an organized, highly selected, narrative format. The transcripts and notes gathered during a research project can easily cover a thousand pages or more, especially if participant-observation is the primary mode. Out of this, the researcher is to seek the essence and present it so that the reader might also capture the significant heart of this human experience as it came from the participants—all in a few pages!

The analysis section can be divided into several subsections. If the *setting* of the experience is unique and significant, a description is offered so that the reader might have this physical, visual context to understand the unique experience which occurs within it. Studies which deal with a prison, and inner-city school or a Polish ghetto might offer the reader some detail of this setting by describing the author's first entry into that environment, or a special event which took place during the study signifying its character, or simply a detailed description communicating its flavor as well as its physical makeup. Frequently, this will be an entire chapter in itself.

*Profiles* of the participants become helpful to the reader in studies where interviewing was the primary mode. While using pseudonyms to keep them anonymous, these profiles can introduce the character as well as the significant demographic details of the participants. If the number of participants is low, the reader will then be able to visualize and catch their personality behind some of the quotes of the subsequent subsection, heightening the sense of engaging the experience of the participants. These profiles should tell the stories of the participants, flavored with several of their own quotations and anecdotes, at least as these relate to the experience under study. Some researchers will use profiles as the main organizing format for the presentation of their material while others feel that this shifts the reader's attention away from understanding the focal topic. Again, these profiles may become a chapter of the report in itself.

The primary chapter of the analysis section is the *categorical* or *thematic* analysis. The objective here is not only to present selectively the significant material, but to look at the focal experience thread by thread. The experience related by the participants is broken down into its elements and these are organized into about seven categories which together make up the whole experience. Sometimes these categories are predetermined by the literature and/or the questions of a structured interview. Sometimes they emerge from the material as the researcher comes to identify them in the meaning-making process. They may be chronological stages in the experience, or logical categories, or merely various facets or aspects of a complex experience. In any case, they will be parts of a whole and, together, represent all the significant elements of the experience under study.

Once these several themes have been determined, the researcher will gather and distribute the significant material under each of these themes. Looking at the first theme and reviewing all the participant's material, the researcher will seek to understand and tell the story of that theme, in her or his own words but representing the experience as faithfully as possible. Then, the researcher will return to the story line and insert the best, most illustrative quotations and anecdotes into the story so that approximately half of the material is from the participants and half from the researcher. To the reader, it will seem as if the chapter comes from the chorus of participants and the researcher telling the connecting story is merely a coordinating voice in the background.

These quotations can appear as single sentences within a narrative paragraph, or as major block quotations following a commentary point, or even as one- or two-word expressions unique to a participant within a sentence. Unless it is a major point made for emphasis, several quotations would not be strung one after another. They are as much part of the flow of the storytelling as they are documentation of points already made.

The analysis section of the report, then, presents the material in a selective, organized manner, category by category. It looks at the experience piece by piece rather than as a whole and in the participants' own words rather than from the researcher's voice. This is somewhat in contrast to the synthesis section.

### Synthesis Report

This section of the report is the fruit of the entire research effort. It answers the questions: What does it all mean? How can I understand this human experience? This is the researcher's own interpretation or theory and is spoken in his or her voice with few or no quotations from the participants. The individual threads of the analysis section are rewoven back into the tapestry where the unifying form is clearly revealed. (Note that qualitative researchers use many terms interchangeably to describe this verbal characterization of this human experience: interpretation, synthesis, theory, analogy, paradigm, gestalt, form, meaning, significance.) A successful synthesis has several characteristics: it is analogical, simple, memorable, clear, and universal, in short, resonant to the reader's own experience, however far removed that might be from the topical experience. When possible, all of these are achieved by a metaphorical synthesis.

Essentially, any interpretation or theory of a human experience is analogical. Human experiences are highly complex and we can never totally fathom either their psychological depths nor cultural complexities. Even if we could, the other person's experience will never be exactly the same as ours through which we comprehend it. We know by analogy. Experience X is very much like Y; essentially different but, in many of its characteristics, like Y. All theories, even scientific theories, are analogical characterizations.

To be successful, to help us understand this complex human experience, our analogy must be simple and memorable. *Pregnanz*, the term used by the

Gestalt Psychologists to describe this quality, also contains the characteristic of latent depth. A good theory can embrace as much or as little of the complexity of the phenomenon as it chooses, but if it embraces too much, then the reader, rather than having a good grasp of the experience, is overwhelmed and lost and still does not understand. The analogy must lend itself to being grasped as a whole, as one single phenomenon.

Moreover, it must be memorable. An analogy must have qualities which the reader knows well and can identify with. It must be imaginable, have some personal quality, or some visual, sensual, or feeling element. Finally, an effective analogy should not be purely cognitive but have some human, experiential qualities with which the reader can resonate, unconsciously if not consciously. You can see that these three characteristics, simplicity, memorability, and depth, are not discrete items but that one is implicit in the other.

Reviewing the past works of qualitative researchers, I have noticed that some of these analogies are built in from the very beginning. Many experiences can be described in the analogy of a game with certain players, rules, penalties, strategies, and goals. The analogy of a drama is often used with roles—initial problem, ascending conflict, and final resolution. Often primary cultural metaphors are used to describe a particular experience, especially that of progressive evolution or developmental analogies. The experience is described linearly, broken into phases and each seen as a growth or development of the previous one, moving to some yet-unspecified growth culmination. American developmental psychology depends heavily upon this analogy, in contrast to Russian psychology, which draws on environmental and sociological analogies.

Myths have provided us with very effective metaphors. Freud and Jung were quite fond of using Greek mythology to describe human experience—the Oedipal complex, narcissism. Today, we are familiar with the Peter Pan Syndrome, Cinderella Complex, the Inner Child, and the Impostor Syndrome, all metaphors used as syntheses for various researchers' discoveries.

Often our research does not approach this metaphorical level of interpretation and our theory of what this experience means must remain on a lower, more prosaic level. Just how simple, memorable, or experiential we can make our interpretation is relative. Nevertheless, our responsibility is to perceive the experience as a whole, to develop a particular, unifying perspective, and be able, narratively, to share this view with the reader in the synthesis section.

*Commentary*

While it is not essential to the task, your reader would be disappointed if, having engaged this experience with such depth and developed all this insight and expertise, you leave without sharing some of your acquired wisdom. And you would be an unusual researcher if, during the weeks and months of your endeavor, you did not have several meditations about the value and implications of your discovery. The final section of your project provides a platform for such a discussion. The commentary is usually on a single topic, but it may even deal with two or more. The reader, however, usually prefers development and depth of ideas over more superficial, almost ritualistic statements about limitations and future research.

The most common topic for discussion is the implications of your discovery for clinical practice, whatever that might mean for your particular audience. Given this insight, this better understanding of a problematic human experience, how might we as professionals better approach those under our care? How have we been misunderstanding or missing the mark? Given this understanding, how can we be more empathic and more responsive?

Often our grounded research opens up knowledge about which the literature has either been quite silent or (coming from its more theoretical point of view) presented quite different opinions. Offering the reader a dialogue with the literature is very engaging. Are there differences in perceptions? Has your research added to, or confirmed, or enhanced what we know already about this experience? Given our professional or research concerns, where should we go from here in our inquiry?

Sometimes, your research method in itself will result in some interesting discoveries. You may discover an effective way to engage children that has not been reported before, or a combination of individual and group interviewing which brings surprising results. Or you may have experienced a particular disaster in your process that you were not warned about. Ordinarily, this would go in the methodology section of your final version, but unusual discoveries might better be discussed in this commentary section.

## The Process of Meaning Making

The preceding picture of the three sections which deal with the results of your research—the analysis, synthesis, and commentary sections—was given first to avoid any confusion between their content and the involved process which leads to their development. But now, what is this prior process of meaning making which makes these three sections possible?

In chapter 11, I noted that some prefer more organized, structured approaches to qualitative research, while others prefer more responsive, oscillating approaches. This same continuum is found in the processing phase as well—a more structured and a more interactive method. Both are ancillary, supporting the mind's interpretive thinking process; neither produces analytic themes or a synthetic interpretation of itself. But given the massive amount of material and the enormous extent of the task, the support of one or the other is necessary.

The more structured approach begins with the completed transcript. All extraneous "chit-chat" within the material is eliminated and the researcher begins identifying each unit of thought, whether it be a sentence or a paragraph, and assigning to each unit a code, a word or two identifying its unique, essential idea or topic. As the researcher works through the first and then subsequent interviews, standard codes are developed and some major ideas begin to appear with frequency. Isolates are set aside and the repeated codes are listed. If the result of this coding is, let us say, 128 different code words through the entire set of interviews or other material, the researcher will next search through them and their represented material to identify combining units, umbrella themes under which several codes can be organized. If appropriate to the material, combining the coding into about five to nine themes would be desirable.

From here, two converse movements occur. On one hand, the researcher will study the identified themes to see if there is an overarching concept which makes the newly identified themes participating parts of a whole. Is there an overarching concept emerging? Do all the themes suggest this concept? Do some of the themes stand a bit peripheral to this concept? At this point, some reappraisal and negotiating takes place among the codes, the themes, and the overarching concept to identify a cohesive organization. A balance is conscientiously maintained between being faithful to the material and the mind of the participants and identifying a coordinating perspective. The overarching concept which emerges from this activity becomes the core of the synthesis and, at some point, is taken up for further development.

Intermittent with this activity of working upward to develop an overarching concept is the converse movement to work downward, to begin developing the individual themes. All the codings and their materials are separated out of their original interviews and reassembled into their thematic groupings. This is usually done mechanically, either on the computer or by cutting up the interview transcripts and re-sorting them into files, one for each theme.

Once reorganized into themes, the different coded materials within each theme are again sorted into their individual coded units. The codes themselves are arranged into an outline of some sequential or logical continuum—into a story line—as it appears appropriate to the researcher and to the central concept. Utilizing this outline, the researcher then takes the coded material in the outline's sequence and constructs a narrative of its contents. Selected representative materials—quotations and anecdotes—are set within the narrative intermittently. When this task has been completed in each of the themes, a rewrite and editing occurs to smooth out the continuity, cohesion, and literary communication. The result is the analysis chapter.

Returning to the overarching concept, the researcher hopefully is ready to transcend the somewhat piecemeal mechanized approach of the thematic analysis and to develop a full, detailed explication of the grounded theory of this human experience. This becomes the synthesis chapter.

Those who favor this more structured approach have had some success using computers to facilitate its process. *The Ethnograph* for IBM and *HyperQual* and *HyperRESEARCH* for the Macintosh, among several other programs, are capable of coding the text, developing a list of codes for identification and reorganization, and reorganizing the codes and materials as the codes are grouped into themes and outlined under each theme.

The alternative process for the identification of meaning is more recursive and unfolding than the structured approach just described. But keep in mind, as was noted with the interviewing methods, there are as many variations of these two extremes as there are researchers and research efforts. These two approaches are polarized types rather than directives to be precisely followed. For the sake of convenience and clarity, I would like to label the first approach the "grounded theory" method, and label this approach the "hermeneutical" method—but only for the convenience of this conversation.

The researcher of the hermeneutical persuasion is preoccupied with the questions: What does this mean? What is the meaning of human experience which is unfolding before me? She or he will begin reading the first transcription and accompanying notes, recording whatever meanings may occur to her or him about what this person is communicating and the experience which underlies that communication. In the analysis of the first interview, these side annotations may be more in the nature of questions, possibilities, and curiosities than possible meanings, but the main characteristic is that of dialoguing with the transcribed materials and the memory of the actual interview itself.

As the investigator moves on to the materials from the second and third interviews, these annotations will begin to link the interviews and the emergent meanings they share in common. Possible common meanings will begin to appear alongside annotations of continuing curiosities and potential linkages. In small ways, the dialogue will begin to bear fruit. But for this very reason, the hermeneutical researcher will develop a healthy suspicion of new insights and will carefully test them against the new material review: Are there other possible interpretations? Would another researcher see this material in another way?

Keep in mind that the hermeneutical researcher (assuming a consistent style) will be interviewing or engaging the field while analyzing. His or her probing mind, searching for meaning, will be engaging this quest with each new interview as well as with each new transcript. The dialogue and annotations of emergent meaning will not only be engaging the transcripts, but the participants as well. This circle of thought and conversation, reflection and engagement, and its accompanying pervading question—What does this mean?—will be experienced as a growing tension, a physical and emotional tension, as more material is reviewed and compared, and as the annotations accumulate and become more and more interconnected. Then, at some point in the process, there is that "a ha!" experience of the gestalt coming together.

As I write it, this paragraph just completed, and especially the last sentence, sounds like magical thinking, and I would be tempted to doubt it myself if I had not experienced it in my own research and with many of my students in their research. It does not always occur. It never occurs in my one-semester, two-credit research course, and it seldom bows to university deadlines. A high degree of depth immersion and abiding in the experience is requisite. Successful students report that, consciously or unconsciously, they have lived with their study night and day for several weeks and months. Given this level of involvement, the gestalt shift always occurs.

A simplified description of the hermeneutical approach is a recursive pattern of in-depth involvement with the material in whatever form, followed by careful writing out of whatever understandings occur, and then a return to further involvement. With the final discovery of a paradigm of explanation will also come identified themes and the story line which explicates each. The enfolded quotations and anecdotes will follow the same pattern as that of the grounded theory approach.

In addition to the basic writing-out process, researchers have discovered other strategies which help loosen a stuck situation. Some will sit down and talk to a friend who is a good listener or have that friend read some of the transcripts and the two of them share a conversation about their hunches and insights. Some will, mid-process, give a summary talk to a group of colleagues followed by an open discussion.

If the stuck experience is not that you lack an interpretation, but, to the contrary, find yourself tightly locked into a previous interpretation, then find a "set-breaker"—a situation or person who has had a totally different experience, a friend who comes from a different academic or professional perspective, or some exception to your established theory.

This completes your research process. You have gathered your materials and uncovered their meaning. You have stated in writing your focal quest, your conceptual foundation, and your methodological journey. Then you have selectively reported your material, thematically arranged and articulated and expressed your interpretation of the experience under study. Finally, you have added your comments on the significance of these findings. The one remaining task is to write up and communicate your discovery for the benefit of your colleagues and your wider audience. This is the topic of a short, final chapter.

# 13

# Communicating Your Discovery

The heart of the research is complete; you have gathered your materials and have interpreted their meaning. The discovery process that you set out for yourself has been accomplished. Yet one final, crucial task remains before you can lay your work to rest—communicating your discovery to your colleagues and to the larger audience that will benefit from your efforts.

Qualitative research is essentially a social dialogue. Much of our human experience is understandable to us and we quietly engage it in our everyday living. But there are a few troublesome experiences around the edge, within ourselves and in our environment, which we do not understand and which become problematic to us. What are they and how do we deal with them? These become the focal questions of qualitative research.

In response to this discomfort, we systematically engage these human curiosities to name them, to discover their meaning, and then to place this new understanding appropriately within our cognitive map of reality. The result of this learning process is that our lives become more integrated and we are able to engage our social environment more gracefully and purposefully. Each piece of qualitative research, then, becomes a contribution to the personal growth and the well-being of not only ourselves but our fellow human travelers—only, however, if our discovery is shared and communicated to others who find that same set of experiences problematic.

True, your discovered understanding will always be relative and incomplete. The analogy you have used to name this ineffable human experience will not be the final word and there will always be a call for others to build upon and further clarify the experience by offering their perspectives, by extending insight, by revealing other facets. This is highly desirable, the epitome of human conversation. And, as in any human conversation, each advance of the dialogue depends upon the previous contribution. There is genuine social need for you to communicate your discovery to enable this human conversation to advance. Buber defines this as our share in the creation of the world.

All of this speaks to the primary issue of motivation: Why write up your results, why communicate, why publish? Once you are persuaded that communication is a natural part of your research process rather than a presumptive addendum, we can move on to the secondary issue of how this is to be done. I have placed the motivational issue first simply because it is here, and not in the realm of "how to," that most qualitative research fails to enter into the human conversation.

## The Report

The style of your report, in keeping with the manner of qualitative work itself, is not to persuade, document, or prove your findings before a critical audience, but rather to recreate an experience for and engage a concerned audience with the same discovery process in which you engaged in the study yourself. Up to this point, you have been the *student* of this experience— listening, observing, attempting to reach understanding yourself. Now, in this report, you transfer roles and become the *teacher* (or better yet, the *guide*), leading your readers through the same stages of your experience which you traced, showing them (albeit in an organized, simplified manner), and having them experience the same discovery process as you experienced.

Your qualitative audience does not want to be told; they want to be shown. They do not want information, but understanding. They do not want a cognitive statement of your conclusion and an argument persuading them of its validity, but rather an organized, contextual, selective engagement of the experience itself. And, out of that, they want to co-discover with you the meaning you arrived at identifying that experience.

Jacques Barzun (1985) describes the unique style of qualitative work in the image of a jeweled necklace. You, the researcher, have gone out and gathered an assortment of rough, dirt-encrusted stones. After carefully cleaning, cutting, and polishing each of them, you arrange them by size and shape into a beautiful, symmetrical necklace. Your audience admires the necklace's beauty, noting that each jewel perfectly complements the others and that they, in their beauty, could hardly be presented in any other fashion.

The final writing phase begins when the meaning of the experience becomes quite clear in your mind and you understand the phenomenon well enough to be able to explain it as a whole to another person. Before you lies each section of your writing—the focal question, the literature, the methods, the analysis, the synthesis, and the commentary sections. The task is to integrate these units into an unfolding narrative experience which will reveal your discovery to your reader.

Using each of the parts, you want to lay out a guided path along which your readers can retrace your journey and arrive, with you, at the "a ha!" of your conclusion. Obviously, the journey you lay our will be much more expedient than that which you experienced. Each piece and each step will fit perfectly and lead naturally into the next. The jungle you had to hack through will appear like a garden path to your audience.

The binding thread of your report is the analogy or metaphor you have identified. Frequently, it is indicated in the subtitle and then hinted at throughout via sectional headings, figures of speech, and analogies used in the text. *Hinting* is an appropriate term to use here. The writer negotiates a delicate balance, neither announcing his or her interpretation and propagandizing the readers with it repeatedly, nor so confusing the readers with unorganized material that they are utterly lost. In the former instance, the readers feel pushed by the writer and react with resentment and disbelief, seeking to reject the author's interpretation and search for their own. In the latter case, the readers will find the chaos intolerable and construct their own interpretations in the absence of the researcher's.

Contextual descriptions are of major importance in recreating the experience. Details of the setting, the emotional tenor of the conversations, the body language and personal reactions, various visual, aural, and other sense material—all are quite important to enable readers to identify with the experience in their own minds. This accumulation of contextual details lays the foundation for the interpretive understanding at the end.

## Criteria

A successful qualitative report must incorporate the two criteria of clarity and credibility. Clarity depends upon the reader's unambiguous understanding of both the question proposed by the researcher in the beginning of the study and the resolving interpretation provided at the end. Clarity is enhanced when the reader is well guided from section to section, knowing exactly what the author is attempting to deliver and what contribution each section makes to the overall task. To the reader, the report communicates itself as well-organized and clearly structured.

Credibility comes when the report gives the readers confidence in the researcher's maturity, honesty, and skill. They know just who the author is and where he or she stands in relation to the participants and experiences in the report. They sense the careful accuracy, ethical sensitivity and especially the human respect the author demonstrates toward the participants. The author genuinely appears to be an open and appreciative student of the experience without hidden preconceptions, value judgments, or political motives. At no point do the readers feel their trust in the author's honesty has been violated.

In sum, transforming your engagement and understanding of this human experience into a permanent narrative brings your research to its full fruition. Writing a report out for others to read is a great clarifier of your own thinking, but the greater enrichment comes when others do read it and respond with new insights and added energy. Reframing each stage of your research journey into a whole and articulating the entire experience as a single phenomenon completes the journey.

## Publication

The word *publication* often breathes mystification, awe, and fear into the average researcher. Some publish their dissertations in Ann Arbor, Michigan as part of their doctoral program requirement, but usually they are given little direction or expectation beyond this point. Yet, so long as the desire to publish is fostered by a desire to communicate with colleagues and not to fulfill an edict to publish or perish, various paths are available and the mystery can be dissolved (Dorn, 1985; Mullins, 1977; Perry, 1991).

A careful study of your media is important and requires a bit of library research. The usual media for qualitative research are dissertations, professional magazines, scholarly journals, and trade books. The middle two present article-length reports but are quite distinct. Professional magazines present to a wider audience and are more literary and popular in their presentations. Scholarly journals are more academic, formal, and specific in their presentations to a scholarly audience.

Major libraries have in their reference sections various publishing directories such as the *Directory of Publishing Opportunities in Journals and Periodicals*, or APA's *Journals in Psychology: A Resource Listing for Authors*. Within each directory you can locate those publications which publish in your topic area, the required style and details of submission, and the name and address for your submission. From there, locate that magazine within the library and review some of the issues and articles it publishes.

If the publication looks like the appropriate medium for your research, then you follow one of two paths. If the magazine is a scholarly journal, you send the required number of copies of your article in the specified format to the journal which seems the most appropriate. You may submit to only one journal at a time. At refereed journals, articles being initially considered are submitted to two or more experts for independent evaluation. The turnaround time for a decision can be slow.

On the other hand, if you select one or several professional publications, then your initial step is to send query letters to all of them simultaneously, briefly telling them of your focal question and the results of your research, possibly adding an outline of your article, noting the audience and interest your research would attract, and asking if their publication would have an interest in reviewing your research report. Those publications whose current editorial or reader interests are focusing on your topic area will respond with an invitation to submit your full article. Again, follow their style requirements and make your submissions one at a time.

Well-known publications and journals receive large numbers of submissions and the odds of acceptance are low. If you receive a rejection letter, don't bother to nurture a bruised ego; resubmit to another journal immediately. However, there are several newer, lesser-known publications which publish in specialty areas. These are not inundated with submissions and should not be overlooked in your search. You are not looking for fame and fortune in this business but for those select colleagues who want to be a part of your professional conversation.

## Example

In summary, one way of tying together the last five chapters is to offer a brief synopsis of one such research effort. In a recent dissertation Frances Turnbull took as her *focal question* the adjustment reactions of twenty-four men and women who lost a parent between the ages of seven and seventeen. These deaths were premature and occurred through illness, accident, or suicide. For a *theoretical perspective* through which to look at this experience, she chose the mourning process from childhood developmental literature. She *gathered* her material through individual, semistructured interviews, which she modified according to each participant's needs. The material was *analyzed* thematically, revealing those experiences held in common, but also the unique experiences around the type of death and the age of the child when the death occurred. In her *interpretation*, Frances found that parent loss resulted for all her participants in an alteration of their sense of self, a loss of innocence, and an end of childhood. Adjustment was described by most as a lifelong process but it resulted in an increased acceptance of death and loss and a renewed sense of purpose in life.

## Conclusion

This brings us to the end of our discovery process. The qualitative approach is a research method, one among many, but it can be argued that it is much more than "just research." Martin Buber, the Jewish existentialist, defines qualitative process as part of that human dialogue through which one human being's experience is "made present" to another. When the other becomes present to me, I confirm him or her in their being. I enable them to become that unique person which he or she has always been called to be. "A society may be termed human in the measure to which its members confirm one another," Buber observed in *The Knowledge of Man*. "It is from one person to another that the heavenly bread of self-being is passed."

# Epilogue

There is a familiar saying that if all you have is a hammer, everything begins to look like a nail. A major purpose of this book has been to invite the reader to see beyond the nails and the use of the hammer in reflecting upon and preparing for research. The researcher has been encouraged to think about different paradigms for research as well as a methodological pluralism. We have been interested in breaking any monolithic, absolutistic or fundamentalist mind-set about research. We have sought to affirm Polkinghorne's view that "the crucial shift made in post-positivism is away from a unified view of science and a unified methodology of research and a move towards using whatever research approaches are responsive to the particular questions raised and subject matters addressed" (1983).

Diverse conceptions of research methodology are necessary in human science research. In the advancement of an expanded human science methodology, a key issue is what the best possible fit is between the research problem and the research methods to be utilized. We need to utilize a wide variety of research methods, but we need to use them prescriptively so that the best methods are chosen to investigate the problem that is being studied. Sometimes a research problem clearly needs either a quantitative or a qualitative approach, and there are occasions when various aspects of knowledge about a problem can best be garnered by using mixed methods of research. Hopefully, as pastoral caregivers venture more courageously into using research to expand the knowledge and practice of our field, they will experience a benediction to their creativity and rigorous quality in using diverse methodologies.

It has been noted that scientific research and religion have much in common since both of them try to explore mystery and to expand knowledge.

Unfortunately, there has too often been a tendency in both areas to claim an absolute knowledge of the truth as well as the means for getting at that truth. Claims of inerrancy both in interpreting Scripture and in supposedly "scientific" method have set up false absolutes. These in turn have closed off the human mind from continuing to explore from a faith orientation that which has been shrouded in mystery. May the pastoral arts and sciences through their expanding commitment to research continue to deepen respect for both mystery and for the various ways of discovering knowledge and truth.

# References

Aquinas, T. (1964). *Summa theologia*. Thomas Gilbey, Trans.. New York: McGraw Hill. Vol. 1, pp. 1-2.

Augustine, St. (1957). *The confessions of Saint Augustine*. Edward Pussey, Trans. New York: Pocket Library.

Augustine, St. (1963). *The trinity*. Stephan McKenna, Trans. Washington, DC: Catholic University Press of America.

Barbaria, J. (1993). *The historical and philosophical foundations of qualitative research*. Unpublished manuscript.

Barzun, J. (1985). *The modern researcher*. HBJ College Pubs.

Briod, M. (1992, June). Opening statement to the 11th International Human Science Research Conference. Richmond, MI.

Buber, M. (1988). *The knowledge of man*. Humanities.

Carnap. R. (1963). *Logical foundations of probability*. Chicago: University of Chicago Press.

Dibielius, M. (1956). The first Christian historian. In *Studies of the Acts of the Apostles*. London: SCM Press.

Dilthey, W. (1883). *Einleitung in die Geisteswissenschaften*. Leipzig: Dunchker and Hujbolt.

Dorn, F. J. (1985). *Publishing for professional development*. Muncie, IN: Accelerated Developments.

Dowdy, S. & Wearden, S. (1991). *Statistics for research*. New York: John Wiley.

Flew, A. & MacIntyre, A. (Eds.). (1955). *New essays in philosophical theology*. New York: Macmillan.

Giorgi, A. (1970). *Psychology as a human science. A Phenomenological based approach*. New York: Harper & Row.

Glaser, B. and Strauss, A. (1967). *The Discovery of Grounded Theory*. Chicago: Adline.

Guba, E. & Lincoln, Y. (1989). *Fourth generation estate*. Newbury Park, CA: Sage.

Kuhn, T. (1970). *The structure of scientific revolutions*. Chicago: University of Chicago Press.

Mainwaring, L. M. (1991). *Metatheoretical diversity and organizing principles for human inquiry*. Unpublished paper.

Mishler, E. G. (1986). *Research interviewing: Context and narrative*. Cambridge: Harvard University Press.

Mitchell, B. (1955). Theology and falsification. In A. Flew and A. MacIntyre (Eds.). *New essays in philosophical theology*. New York: Macmillan.

Moustaskas, C. (1990). *Heuristic research—Design, methodology, and applications*. Newbury Park, CA: Sage.

Mullins, Carolyn J. (1977). *A guide to writing and publishing in the social and behavioral sciences*. New York: John Wiley.

Ong, W. J. (1982). *Orality and literacy: The technologizing of the Word*. New York: Methuen.

Pannenberg, W. (1976). *Theology and the philosophy of science*. Philadelphia: Westminster.

Peabody, F. (1927). The care of the patient. *Journal of the American Medical Society, 88*, 879.

Perry, Carol R. (1991). *The fine art of technical writing*. Hillsboro, OR: Blue Haron Press.

Polanyi, M. (1985). *Personal knowledge*. Chicago: University of Chicago Press.

Polanyi, M. (1964). *Science, faith, and society*. Chicago: University of Chicago Press.

Polkinghorne, D. (1983). *Methodology for the human sciences*. Albany, NY: State University of New York Press.

Popper, K. (1963). *Conjectures and refutations*. London: Routledge & Kegan Paul.

Reinharz, Shulamet. (1992). *Feminist methods in social research*. New York: Oxford University Press.

Russell, B. (1927). *An outline of philosophy*. New York: Meridian.

Schleiermacher, F. (1966). *Brief outline of the study of theology*. T. N. Tite, Trans. Richmond, VA: John Knox.

Schweitzer, A. (1948). *The quest for the historical Jesus*. New York: Macmillan.

Southard, S. (1976). *Religious Inquiry*. Nashville: Abingdon Press.

Strauss, A. & Corbin, Juliet. (1990). *Basics of qualitative research*. Newbury Park, CA: Sage.

Strunk, O., Jr. (1989). Research in the pastoral arts and sciences: A reassessment. *Journal of Pastoral Psychotherapy, 2*, 3-12.

Taylor, S. J., & Bogdan, R. (1984). *Introduction to qualitative methods: The search for meaning*. New York: John Wiley.

Torrance, T. F. (1969). *Theological science*. New York: Oxford University Press.

Zeigler, P. (1969). *The black death*. New York: Torchbook.

# Index

2 2 5.5 0 7
V.2 35

252.507
V225

LINCOLN CHRISTIAN COLLEGE AND SEMINARY

89590

252.507 V225                    89590
VandeCreek, Larry.
Research in pastoral care
 and counseling

DEMCO